T0083577

# Miroslav Vaněk

# Around the Globe

# Rethinking Oral History with Its Protagonists

Charles University in Prague
Karolinum Press 2013

Reviewed by:
PhDr. Pavel Urbášek
PhDr. Pavel Mücke, Ph.D.


*This publication was created as part of the following project:*
*Czech Society during the "Normalization" and Transformation*
*Period: Biographical Narratives (GA CZ Reg. No. P410/11/1352).*

ISBN 978-80-246-2226-2

Acknowledgements

*I would like to thank all those narrators and oral historians, who found the time to be interviewed during hectic international conferences and at other times and thus helped to create this book. I would also like to thank all my colleagues at the Oral History Center of the Academy of Science of the Czech Republic's Institute of Contemporary History for their invaluable consultation, and especially Lenka Krátká for her preparation of all necessary materials and editing work on the interviews.*

Miroslav Vaněk

# Content

# 1/ Preface

The publication *On Oral History with Its Founders and Protagonists*[1] was an initial attempt to introduce to the Czech public important international figures in the field of oral history, including their personal recollections and, above all, their views reflecting upon fundamental theoretical-methodological questions in our field. The decision to publish interviews with those who stood at the starting point of oral history's modern tradition and with those currently influencing this multidisciplinary field on an international scale seemed to me in 2008 to be both inspirational and necessary. I was led to this decision by the undisputable fact that various oral historians from sundry universities and academic institutions on several continents have profoundly influenced the work of Czech oral historians, and in many ways their publications have helped them push through a new (and thus considered "dubious" in the Czech milieu) method. Oral history's path was completely blocked off during the communist regime and encountered difficulties even after 1989.[2] The process of recognizing oral history in the Czech Republic (as in all former Eastern Bloc countries) could be likened to the now legendary pos-

---

1) Vaněk, Miroslav: *O orální historii s jejími zakladateli a protagonisty* (On Oral History with Its Founders and Protagonists). Prague, The Academy of Science of the Czech Republic's Institute of Contemporary History 2008.
2) Vaněk, Miroslav: *Orální historie ve výzkumu soudobých dějin* (Oral History in the Research of Contemporary History). Prague, The Academy of Science of the Czech Republic's Institute of Contemporary History 2004. Vaněk, Miroslav – Mücke, Pavel – Pelikánová, Hana: *Naslouchat hlasům paměti: Teoretické a praktické aspekty orální historie.* (Listen to the Voices of Memory: Theoretical and Practical Aspects of Oral History). Prague, The Academy of Science of the Czech Republic's Institute of Contemporary History 2007. Vaněk, Miroslav – Mücke, Pavel: *Třetí strana trojúhelníku. Teorie a praxe orální historie* (The Triangle's Third Side. Theory and Practice in Oral History). Prague, The Faculty of Humanities of Charles University – Prague, The Academy of Science of the Czech Republic's Institute of Contemporary History 2011.

tulate by German philosopher Arthur Schopenhauer concerning the three phases of accepting new discoveries and methods by the relevant field or, as the case may be, by society. Oral history too passed through an initial phase of ridicule, a second phase of being violently opposed to, and suddenly emerged in the phase of being accepted as self-evident.

In 2012, the Karolinum publishing house offered to publish the book in English. I wavered on whether to accept this offer or not. On the one hand, I liked the idea that an English version would make the interviews accessible to a broader public. This would certainly be appreciated by my colleagues from countries that experienced circumstances similar to those of the Czech Republic (possibly even other countries as well). On the other hand, I was faced with the task of once again asking the narrators to edit and authorize the English text and knew that this could entail a relatively long process. Yet I was mistaken in this. For the most part my narrators (whom I now dare call my friends) reacted immediately.

Some of the narrators had already nearly forgotten about our interview and were surprised that I had "found" this kind of text. Others, in authorizing the interview, pointed out the increasingly complex issue that oral history embodies, whether we are speaking of questions of a theoretical-methodological, interpretational or ethical nature. It was for these reasons, as well as others that I will mention later, that I decided to take advantage of this renewed communication with my colleagues to broaden the original interviews so that they included responses (this time, however, only in the form of email correspondence) to current questions regarding oral history that I had not considered to be overly important six years ago.[3] In my view, this attests to one thing: oral history is in the Czech milieu (though obviously elsewhere too) a dynamically evolving field/method of research.

The focus of this study and the aim of these published interviews is certainly not an attempt to create a partial "history of oral his-

---

3) On the other hand, the English version of the publication does not contain parts of the interviews that were edited out for thematic reasons but released on DVD along with the Czech version.

tory", nor is it an attempt to answer basic theoretical questions that we are presently posing and will only receive possible answers to in the future (e.g. questions regarding the influence of globalization on the development, forms and tasks of oral history or the dilemma of whether oral history should be considered a research method or a scientific field).[4] Rather, the objective of this work is to show how internationally prominent researchers, whose work has contributed significantly to the development of oral history, can differ in their views on current and future themes concerning oral history. Yet this heterogeneity of specific views and positions does not divert them from their common goal, which is to develop oral history in historiography and the other social sciences. At the same time, I would like to convey to all my colleagues and, above all, to those studying the humanities an authentic view of the founders and pioneers of oral history. In this spirit, I also hope to inspire them to reflect upon the perspectives and paths that they themselves would like to take if they opt to pursue oral history research.

Just ten years ago I would have considered the chance for me to ask questions to the founders and main protagonists in the field, the very people whom I had known up to that point only through their texts, as more of a fairytale. I still recall the thrill from the first articles and publications written by leading figures in oral history as I literally devoured their ideas on issues in contemporary oral history, its possible crossroads and pitfalls, its future in a globalized world and, finally, its possible use in interdisciplinary research.

Quite a few years have elapsed since that, I dare say fateful (at least for me), meeting when I decided to conduct the interviews (the interviews were conducted in 2007–2008). During that time, several

---

4) Many more qualified individuals have already addressed the history of oral history. See, for instance: Ritchie, Donald A.: *Doing Oral History. A Practical Guide.* Oxford, Oxford University Press 2003; Sharpless, Rebecca: The History of Oral History. In: Charlton, Thomas Lee – Myers, Lois E. – Sharpless, Rebecca M. (eds.): *Handbook of Oral History.* Lanham – New York – Toronto – Oxford, Altamira Press 2006, pp. 19–42; Vansina, Jan: *Oral Tradition as History.* University of Wisconsin Press 1985; Grele, Ronald J. (ed.): *Envelopes of Sound: The Art of Oral History.* Praeger Publishers 1991; Thompson, Paul: *The Voice of the Past: Oral History.* Oxford, Oxford University Press 1978.

important events have occurred in Czech oral history as well as in my professional life. If I were to attempt to name the most significant of these, the list would be headed by the major breakthrough that occurred on my trip to the 14th Conference of the International Oral History Association (IOHA) held in Sydney in 2006.[5] Just five months after the Australian conference and the enriching discussions I took part in with Robert Perks, Alistair Thomson and Donald Ritchie in Sydney, we founded the Czech Oral History Association (The Oral History Center of the Institute of Contemporary History had already existed since 2000) as a platform to associate oral historians from all over the Czech Republic. Oral history was gradually established at universities, in museums and in a wide variety of archives, as well as by amateurs using the method to document family stories or the history of local organizations.

Even though I was the only Czech and probably the only representative of the former Eastern Bloc in Sydney in 2006, a highly visible (even from an international perspective) 14-member group of Czech oral historians set out for the 15th IOHA conference held in 2008 in Guadalajara, Mexico. Things developed even more rapidly from there, as it was in Mexico that the decision was made to hold the next IOHA conference in Prague (!). The Prague conference then welcomed what may have been the largest turnout in the history of our meetings with oral historians from literally all continents attending (434 papers were accepted[6]). In Prague I could personally, at least in symbolic gratitude, dedicate the Czech version of the book

5) Perhaps the greatest impetus for the development of oral history in the Czech Republic came from, in addition to foreign publications, these international conferences. I consider my participation in the conferences organized – both the Oral History Association (Durham 2000, Providence 2005, Oakland 2007, Denver 2011) and the International Oral History Association (in addition to the aforementioned conferences in Sydney 2006, Guadalajara 2008, Prague 2010 and Buenos Aires 2012) – to be important meetings for me with the international oral history community. Of equal importance in my view were the oral history panel discussions that I had the opportunity to attend as part of the European Social Science History Conference in Berlin (2002), Amsterdam (2006), Lisbon (2008), Ghent (2010) and Glasgow (2012).
6) For the sake of comparison, the following gives the number of papers received at the various conferences: 1996, Gothenburg 164; 1998, Rio de Janeiro 179; 2000, Istanbul 21; 2002, Pietermaritzburg (South Africa) 154; 2002, Rome 302; 2006, Sydney 203; 2008, Guadalajara (Mexico) 361; 2010, Prague 434; 2012, Buenos Aires 250 estimated.

*On Oral History with Its Founders and Protagonists* to all those colleagues who had provided me with an interview. To ensure that things were sufficiently symbolic, I presented the book to them from my position as the newly elected president of the IOHA (I still feel it was rather audacious of me to accept such a responsible position).

# 2/ The reason for a book of interviews

*"I believe, and I have said and written many times, that identity doesn't exist without continuity. However, we can only talk about identity in the case of people who know today what they were doing in the past, who guarantee and have responsibility here also for the things they did elsewhere. That is the reason it is so important to understand and study history, that is why oral history is also very important. I learned from my own experience that if I was to force myself – and if I actually did it – to write memoirs or reflections of what I lived through, it would surely be poor and not very precise in comparison with what it would be possible to pick out of me through oral history. If questions are asked by well-informed and devoted people, cognizant of the context and of all the details, it can happen that the object of their attention starts to recall things they wouldn't otherwise have remembered or would never have even imagined to be writing about before."*
Václav Havel, 2008[7]

## RESEARCHERS IN THE ROLE OF NARRATORS
The idea to appeal to my colleagues and prominent figures in the field came about by chance – I would now call it a stroke of luck.[8]

---

7) Archive of the Oral History Center of the Institute of Contemporary History. Interviews collection. A video of the greeting of former dissident, playwrite and president of the Czech Republic Václav Havel presented at the 16th IOHA conference in Guadalajara, Mexico to support the organization of the 17th IOHA conference in Prague for 2010.
8) It was the pioneers of oral history, those who today are forging the main direction of research, who, above all, occupied the epicentre of my interest in interviews. Interviews with several presidents of the OHA and IOHA were recorded. Among the thirteen people interviewed were experts from seven countries: Australia, England, the USA, Canada, Bulgaria, Germany and Italy. All interviews are in video form with transcriptions stored at the Oral History Center of the Academy of Science of the Czech Republic's Institute of Contemporary History, Vlašská 9, Prague 1. See www.coh.usd.cas.cz.

During my month-long stay in the USA in 2007, I planned on recording both the talks given at the 41st Oral History Association (OHA) Conference in Oakland, California and several interviews in nearby San Francisco with musicians from the "hippies" period (for my project on the influence of Anglo-American rock music on Czech society). I was therefore equipped with audiovisual recording technology. It took two long sleepless nights of contemplation for the idea of a kind of "second" study to take root in my mind: Why not try approaching the "big fish" of the oral history world and ask to interview them, since I was already prepared to interview Carlos Santana, Peter Albin and Barry Melton?

Another stroke of luck was that the first oral historian I approached with this project was the extremely accommodating David King Dunaway. Not only did he willingly speak of his experiences, but he helped me in the role of "gatekeeper" to contact other pioneers in the field: Ronald Grele and Charles Morrissey. Approaching colleagues I had met in Sydney in 2006 was then no problem. These individuals included Rina Benmayor, Donald Ritchie and Robert Perks. I had originally intended to use the recorded interviews as the basis for an article in a professional periodical, but gradually began to develop a plan to record interviews with other prominent oral historians. The 7th European Social Science History Conference (ESSHC) held in Lisbon in 2008 provided me with the chance to conduct these interviews. Coincidentally, Elizabeth Millwood from the Southern Oral History Program visited Prague in 2007, and so the project included a representative of one of the largest and oldest oral history research centres in the USA.

It was somewhat more complicated, organizationally speaking, to meet with Paul Thompson, a highly revered figure in the field. Following two months of mutual email and telephone communication, Thompson's book *Voice of the Past* that I was holding served as a recognition signal when I waited for this legend in oral history in a London suburb in front of the Genesis cinema. The interview with Paul Thompson led me to the idea to approach another protagonist in the field, the Italian scholar Alessandro Portelli. My learned colleague Hana Pelikánová was up to the task of recording an interview in Rome with set of questions in Italian.

The imaginary circle of interviews with prominent oral historians was symbolically closed in Guadalajara, Mexico at the 16th IOHA conference right on the day that the International Oral History Association's plenary meeting decided that the next international IOHA meeting would take place in Prague. Fittingly, in a symbolic sense, the final narrator was Alistair Thomson – the outgoing president of this international organization.[9] Even before that, however, we were able to conduct an interview with the renowned Canadian historian Alexander Freund.

The selection of the individuals and discussed themes was, for several reasons, given more by the circumstances (possibilities of meeting abroad and the limited time during busy conferences) than by a previously conceived plan.[10] It more depended on the generations they belonged to: from the real doyens of oral history (Paul Thompson, Ronald Grele, who began under the guidance of Charles Morrissey), to the representatives of the older and middle generation who developed oral history in the 1980s, to the representatives of the

---

9) Pilar Dominguez of Spain then became the new president.

10) I certainly would have liked to record traditional autobiographical narratives by these oral historians. The lack of time (the interviews were often conducted in the "stolen" time during breaks of hectic major conferences), however, only allowed me to focus on a few fundamental questions related to testimony on the nature, principles and perspectives of oral history.
I would have also liked to speak with other oral historians that had significantly influenced our field. This was an impossible task, organizationally speaking, and a never-ending project. The following are some other randomly chosen colleagues whom it would certainly have been worth interviewing: Michael Frisch, Mercedes Villanova, Anna Green, Luisa Passerini, Sean Field, Dan P. Dennis, Joanna Bornat, Megan Hutching, Jennie Hopkins Wilson, Jessica Wiederhorn, Albert Lichtblau, Michelle Winslow, Indira Chowdury, Beth M. Robertson, Jacquelyn Dowd Hall, Graham Smith, Paula Hamilton, Kathryn L. Nasstrom, Todd Moya, Almut Leh, Juan-José Gutiérrez, Helen Klaebe, Regina Fitzpatrick and many others whom my memory fails recalling and who would have definitely contributed to the project. In the meantime, however, other colleagues from neighbouring countries have appeared whose work has revealed them to be enviable interview candidates: They include Monika Vrzgulová of Slovakia, Gelinada Grinchenko of Ukraine and Marta Kurkowska of Poland... Perhaps an occasion will arise in the future for me to conduct interviews with the people comprising the long list that I carry around in my head. Or someone else will do it. I think that a kind of encyclopedia of oral historians would make a very good handbook for many researchers and students in their work. An institution like the IOHA could sponsor this kind of publication.

relatively younger generation, who nevertheless are fully established and proven in their field, or the generation of historians (such as Alexander Freund) that emerged *de facto* in the late 1980s and early 1990s.[11]

Regardless of their age, all the narrators expressed the same interest and enthusiasm for oral history and openness toward new possibilities – both in terms of technology (in recording and preserving interviews) and in the thematic view of the world, whose political and social systems underwent radical changes in the late 1980s and early 90s. A reflection of historical development is interestingly seen in comparing the ideological spectrum of the early research work of the interviewed narrators. For instance, Paul Thompson and Alessandro Portelli, both originally from the "Old World" (continental Europe and Great Britain), claimed that their leftist political convictions led them to oral history. I find it interesting that the terms "right-wing" and "left-wing" are understood differently in civic, democratic societies in which oral history was an expression of leftist beliefs mainly in the sense that it held an interest in people "off the streets", marginalized by the majority society and neglected in hitherto traditional historical research.

As Paul Thompson states, oral history's beginnings in the United States focused on researching the ruling and social elites. This may have provoked an interest and need in its leading researchers to take a look at the other side of the social spectrum and to focus on groups overlooked by historians and ostracized by society. Thompson remembers these early periods as a time when oral historians in America were more like archivists and were "much more interested in great men than ordinary people's lives, although this has greatly changed since then. So we didn't get much from their practice and it was really from sociology and anthropology and other social historians that we worked out how to do oral history".[12] Robert Perks

---

11) Daniela Koleva, for instance, who was born in 1961, when the veterans of oral history were already developing their first projects in the Truman and Kennedy libraries.
12) Archive of the Oral History Center of the Institute of Contemporary History, Interviews collection. Interview with Paul Thompson recorded by Miroslav Vaněk, London, Great Britain, March 2008.

even claims that in Great Britain oral history began to be established in connection with "a radical socialist, feminist movement as part of the social history in the 1960s, but it's become a very wide church now of activity". He does add, however, that today when oral history "is being used by many many disciplines so it's becoming a methodology that is used more widely than we ever anticipated, [...] there's also a sense that oral history has sort of lost its radical edge as a political movement and maybe we need to keep an eye on whether we can keep oral history in the forefront of radical change as a social movement".[13]

The historians arriving in the late 1980s and early 1990s from former Eastern Bloc countries, China and Vietnam were a healthy corrective to the aforementioned leftist view of oral history. For instance, Bulgarian Daniela Koleva's research career was made possible and inspired by the regime changes in 1989 in the former Eastern Bloc countries. The freedom in research that these changes brought also became one of the sources of enthusiasm and positive outlooks to the future.

Even though the positions of the creators and protagonists of contemporary oral history have often been characterized as leftist, they were mainly radical in the sense that they not only thematically, but also methodologically defied the traditional concept of historical examination and enthusiastically paved their own way for historical research. This perhaps was helped (at least to a certain extent) by the fact that practically all colleagues interviewed had become involved in oral history in their youth (even if in the beginning they may not have even been aware that their type of research fell under the heading of oral history), at the very beginning of their professional development.

Another factor that should not be overlooked is that almost a third of the oral historians interviewed began their professional specialization in fields other than history. Rina Benmayor, for instance, began her work as an ethnologist collecting Sephardic ballads,

---

13) Archive of the Oral History Center of the Institute of Contemporary History, Interviews collection. Interview with Robert Perks recorded by Miroslav Vaněk, Oakland, USA, October 2007.

Daniela Koleva studied philosophy and sociology and Alessandro Portelli's path to oral history started with his law studies and passed through modern philology and literature directly to oral history when he began to collect protest and political songs (often accompanied by singers' narratives) at the end of the 1960s. Perhaps this too will contribute to an awareness that oral history is open for multidisciplinary and interdisciplinary use and development.

## SPHERES OF RESEARCH

From the very start of my oral history project it was clear to me that, due to time constraints and the fact that I would not get the chance to have follow-up interviews with the narrators, I would not be able to apply the usual method for recording biographical narrative. I therefore opted for the method of a structured interview that contained five thematic spheres: when and how the interviewees first encountered oral history; what they feel is oral history's main strength; their take on the criticism and critics of oral history; how they see the future of oral history, and, finally, any possible advice they might pass on to Czech oral historians.

The first theme (i.e. the first encounter with oral history) interested me from both a professional and personal perspective. What paths and, in particular, what motivation led these people to oral history? Even though their motives vary, some similar traits are evident. Above all, they share a clear activism, at times even radical stances influenced by the social changes of the 1960s and, especially, the events of 1968.[14] Another important factor is the interviewees' own interest in the studied field, especially in new research methods. Robert Perks, who presently heads the British Library Sound Archives, then speaks of very unique and interesting motivation for using oral history: in his case, it was an enchantment with modern technology, especially with audio-technology, that led to his early interest in oral history.

---

14) Cf. Vaněk, Miroslav – Mücke, Pavel: *Třetí strana trojúhelníku* (The Triangle's Third Side) ... c.d., pp. 71–72.

A second, related question that I posed to the narrators concerned the "power" of oral history in historiography and in the other humanities. In this regard, almost all the interviewees mentioned a specific type of information that oral history provides the researcher with and that the historian cannot find in any other sources of information. This is most likely caused by the fact that oral history researchers focus on social classes and individuals that were previously ignored (were not written about) in traditional historical sources, that were marginalized and, in short, were not recorded by traditionally dominant historiography. In the authoritarian regimes these "peripheral groups" were then completely erased "from history".

Charles Morrissey, one of the founders of oral history, offers an interesting take on the power of oral history: "There are several powers, one of which is obvious: it lets neglected people, neglected by historians, by historical documentation, get into history. So if history is the story of rich and powerful men, it allows poor women to get into the historical record. Secondly, [...] when you go into the interview, you can get someone to evoke the context in which the document was created. [...] With the spoken recollection, which has its frailties – memory plays tricks on all of us – on the other hand, some people can come in and zero in precisely on why something happened the way it did that's quite contrary than the impression you would get from the paper trail. Those are the two primary ones. I'll mention the third as a self-satisfaction, really, and that is: every oral historian, by asking questions, is co-creating a record, and that record wouldn't exist if you didn't exert the initiative to make it happen. So you're causing something to exist for the future that would not exist if you didn't help make it exist. [...] Basically I'm a doorkeeper; I open doors and let people into history. And that's very valuable for the future. I'm a historian with a strong sense of the future needs of historical knowledge."[15]

15) Archive of the Oral History Center of the Institute of Contemporary History, Interviews collection. Interview with Charles T. Morrissey recorded by Miroslav Vaněk, Oakland, USA, October 2007.

Alistair Thomson characterized and structured the power and historical contribution that emerged and developed within the oral history milieu: "So one, it's about unrecorded stories, two, it's about memory as a subject as well as a source, and three? Three and four connect, but three is about empowerment and four is about advocacy and I think they're connected. Three, it was my colleague Joanna Bornat in England who put this pretty well, she said that there was a moment in her oral history career when somebody turned around and said after the interview, 'Thank you for interviewing me.' [...] [S]o I think that on a very personal level the third value of what we are doing is that it makes anybody feel like their story is significant. Both for themselves, and wider. And that connects to what I believe is the fourth value of oral history, which is that just in the same way as it can be empowering for an individual, it can be an empowering thing collectively."[16]

All the interviewees also shared a certain scepticism toward the use of exclusively written sources for their own research. Of high interest here is that none of the interviewed pioneers of oral history ever came out in favour of a single approach to examining the past; all emphasized and emphasize the need for complex and multidisciplinary research. It was accurately expressed by Charles Morrissey: "I was at Berkley, the University of California at Berkley, and, of course, all graduate students in history and related disciplines are taught that you can trust the written word but you cannot trust the spoken word. And I found myself more and more sceptical of the written word in its authenticity, its credibility, in print. And if I went and interviewed somebody, I found there was a story that explained the creation of the document, why it has survived, what significance people have attached to it. And in many cases, the story revised the historian's sense of what is the significance of this, why does this document exist."[17]

---

16) Archive of the Oral History Center of the Institute of Contemporary History, Interviews collection. Interview with Alistair Thomson recorded by Miroslav Vaněk, Guadalajara, Mexico, September 2008.
17) Archive of the Oral History Center of the Institute of Contemporary History, Interviews collection. Interview with Charles T. Morrissey recorded by Miroslav Vaněk, Oakland, USA, October 2007.

Donald Ritchie passes on a similar message to his students when he asks that they take a sceptical approach to all sources (since, for instance, many "memoranda in the government are written not to tell you what happened but to disguise what happened")[18], that they mutually compare and contrast all available sources and even recommends that "if their written sources and your oral sources do not agree, they should not automatically believe that the written source is right".[19] The interviewed oral historians thus expressed the view that was in direct contrast to that attributed to them by their critics, who often give pride of place to written sources over all other sources of information and only consider oral testimony to be a kind of illustration, a second- or even third-rate source.

At least at the beginning of their professional careers, most of our "Western" colleagues were not spared the disputations with those colleagues-historians, for whom the only valued and credible source is written documentation. One exception is Rina Benmayor, who claims to avoid the debate with sceptics and opponents of oral history since she considers such arguments to be insignificant. Since her work is conducted in an interdepartmental milieu where this debate does not play a role, she does not even encounter this kind of opposition. Robert Perks, on the other hand, pointed out in the interview that oral historians have long been on the defensive, defending oral history against critics who warn of the fallibility, selectiveness and unreliability of memory. Yet oral history has been "firmly" established since the 1980s, thanks in particular to the work of Alessandro Portelli and those historians who began to take notice of subjectivity and the relationship between the present and the past. Perks considers it a specific trait, but not a shortcoming of oral history that the way in which people recount their memories differs from the memories as such, since "people vocalize their stories in a particular way to a particular audience on a particular occasion

---

18) Archive of the Oral History Center of the Institute of Contemporary History. Interviews collection. Interview with Donald A. Ritchie recorded by Miroslav Vaněk, Oakland, USA, October 2007.
19) Ibid.

representing a particular identity".[20] He sees a difference between memory and narration and points out that if a story is told multiple times over the course of time, it constantly changes. He then considers these observations on the nature of memory and narrative to be especially important in practicing oral history within the context of former communist regimes.[21]

Ronald Grele, one of the doyens of oral history, assured us that he never felt the need to excuse or defend his position as an oral historian, even when oral history was on the defensive against "traditional" historiography, or assumed an apologetic position (we have the same experience in the Czech Republic) and tried to convince its opponents of its validity and possibilities. His precisely formulated position against conservative opponents of oral history is very inspirational (conservatives would call it radical). For Grele says that it is the oral historians who "are asking important questions. The problem is their [conservative historiographers' – comment of author] asking unimportant questions. [...] The important questions are questions of subjectivity, questions of consciousness, questions of ideology, questions of identity. Those are the important questions. The important questions are not questions of fact; the important questions are not questions of data. The important question is how people live in history, how people create their pasts".[22]

In her position against traditional historians, Daniela Koleva defends oral history by referring to Paul Thompson's aphoristic quote that "the written document has lost its innocence".[23] In her and Elizabeth Millwood's view, the "edges" of the methodological conflict should be "smoothed" so that we are equally critical towards written and oral documents and always critically analyze the context in which sources are created. Daniela Koleva adds that, when speaking

20) Archive of the Oral History Center of the Institute of Contemporary History. Interviews collection. Interview with Robert Perks recorded by Miroslav Vaněk, Oakland, USA, October 2007.
21) Ibid.
22) Archive of the Oral History Center of the Institute of Contemporary History. Interviews collection. Interview with Ronald Grele recorded by Miroslav Vaněk, Oakland, USA, October 2007.
23) Archive of the Oral History Center of the Institute of Contemporary History, Interviews collection. Interview with Daniela Koleva recorded by Miroslav Vaněk, Lisbon, Portugal, February 2007.

of memory, we must not forget the relativity of truth and that "there is no truth with a capital T which is always valid and always the same and to which we are bound to arrive only through rigorous research procedures".[24] Koleva expresses the beliefs also held by other oral historians that oral history will never be and does not strive to be the only privileged source of historical knowledge, whose quality depends, to a considerable extent, on how many different research methods and types of sources it comes from and how many our picture of the past is composed of.[25]

Memory, its selectiveness and the process of remembering and forgetting past events obviously relates to the theme of "truthfulness". A large portion of the interviews was therefore devoted to the theme of memory. Before we take a look at memory in oral history from theoretical positions, let us "listen" to how two prominent oral historians perceive it. Alessandro Portelli does not believe that memory can only get worse in time (a view he considers positivistic and errant), since "[m]emory is not that the facts are there and we can't help forgetting them. Memory is a continuous work. The facts stay there and you keep going – more or less consciously – transforming the meaning in the course of your life, in the course of time. So what it gives us is precisely what the meaning means, what the past means in our present."[26] Ronald Grele refers directly to Portelli in his contemplations on memory: "If you read Portelli the fascinating part of memory is that people don't remember things correctly, you know. Why don't they? What's going on? What is happening? [...] What lies were people telling themselves? What world were they imagining? The world of the imagination? Those are the important questions, I think."[27]

---

24) Ibid.

25) Ibid.

26) Archive of the Oral History Center of the Institute of Contemporary History. Interviews collection. Interview with Alessandro Portelli recorded by Hana Pelikánová, Rome, Italy, May 2008.

27) Archive of the Oral History Center of the Institute of Contemporary History. Interviews collection. Interview with Ronald Grele recorded by Miroslav Vaněk, Oakland, USA, October 2007.

It was the "excessive" subjectivity of oral history (and thus its "unreliability") in "competition" with other sources that caused some to reject it. It is true that the information acquired from individual narratives can hardly be perceived through the prism of quantifying gauges used in working with other types of sources. The interviews come from the individual's past experiences, are influenced by the passage of time and the environment in which they were created, depend on the personal motives of the interviewed, on whom the interview was provided to and many other factors. Therefore, in comparison with other sources, the information obtained in interviews is heavily subjective. We must, however, emphasize that the researcher in oral history does not perceive this attribute to be a disadvantage, but instead sees it as its part and a specific, necessary quality and one of the main reasons why he/she conducts the interviews. It is thus through oral history that the researcher gets new information, findings and views that enrich, expand or corrects his/her hitherto understanding of history. Thanks to the interviewee's experiences and responses, the researcher has the opportunity to provide an individual dimension ("the humanization of history") to his historiography.[28] This is also why the critics of oral history began to gradually accept oral sources as well. Yet the information acquired from interviews certainly should not, at least in our view of oral history, become a kind of illustrative supplement to supposedly objectifying "great" history.

The acquisition of "objective facts", with which the narrator obviously operates in interviews, should not be the main priority of the posed questions and incentive for the narrative, and neither should a heavy emphasis be placed on this (e.g. in the form of judging their "accuracy", "mistakes" or omissions during the ensuing analysis and interpretation of the interview). Yet this appeal has not been fully embraced, for there undoubtedly are historical themes (and projects derived from them) that focus on this (factographic) complementary part of the interview's content. These could be themes or events,

---

28) Vaněk, Miroslav – Mücke, Pavel: *Třetí strana trojúhelníku* (The Triangle's Third Side) ... c.d., p. 20.

about which other "more valid" or "more reliable" types of sources were not preserved or never existed (such as secret conspiratorial meetings "behind closed doors", many sea or air battles or catastrophes, prisoners in prison-of-war or concentration camps and, more generally, the official and non-official past of authoritarian regimes).

Oral history's central interest is to observe a person as a human being by capturing, analyzing and interpreting his verbal and non-verbal communication (e.g. his/her body language or the environment in which the interview is conducted). Since, from an epistemological perspective, all ways of "communicating the past", despite their pros and cons, are equal (from a written document and sculpture of a prominent statesman, to secret police files and a gramophone record, to a poster or email spam), the strict and often artificially polarized difference between so-called objective and subjective historical sources are done away with.[29]

Human subjectivity, which is unique to each of us, to narrators as well as researchers and interpreters (and not only those utilizing oral sources), is aptly documented by a single old legend that shows a different view on reality and the world depending on the life situation at a particular moment. According to this legend, a priest (in some versions he is a sage) asked some men what they were doing at a building site. The first of them said: "I'm making money." The second answered the same question with: "I'm hewing a stone." And a third man proudly replied: "I'm building a cathedral!" It is clear that each person has a unique mix of views and attitudes, and that these cannot be unified. Each of us has some part of the three aforementioned men. Yet the moment the question is posed, each of us emphasizes a different aspect of our personality and different motivation in responding. This motivation can then change during the individual's life depending on external circumstances, social position, health, etc. Clearly, each day is different; sometimes we feel self-contentment, other times disappointment and futility. This is human nature: supremely individual, therefore subjective, and in spite of this, or perhaps because of it, profoundly truthful.

---

29) Ibid.

Many interviews held specific views on the individual and collective memory from a historical, psychological and sociological perspective. In the view of Ronald Grele and Alexander von Plato, we should avoid the trap that is often "set" for oral history, in the form of the assertion that human memory can change, and therefore is worthless for historic research. Alexander von Plato points out that we now know that this is a trap, since oral history is not the reconstruction of hard facts and numbers, and its strongest aspect is the interpretation of living or, better yet, "grasped" history. In his view, oral history enables us to trace the continuity of attitudes, opinions, perceptions, consensual elements and their results, which last much longer than the political and social circumstances that transformed them.[30] We could use the interviews (and their interpretations) with former communist officials and dissidents[31] and, as is proving increasingly the case, with workers during the Normalization (hard-line communist rule during the 1970s) period.[32] A somewhat surprising part of all these interviews shows that the views and opinions of the narrators of the aforementioned groups have endured twenty years after a change occurred in the circumstances that helped create and stabilize these opinions.

In one of his articles, Alexander von Plato points out the fact that those criticizing oral recollected testimony as valid sources in historiography do not want to see that a reduction of the source base to only written sources, in particular to state administration files, is

---

30) Plato, Alexander von: Zeitzeugen und historische Zunft. Erinnerung, kommunikative Tradierung und kollektives Gedächtnis in der qualitativen Geschichtswissenschaft – ein Problemaufriss. *BIOS* 13, 2000, pp. 20–21.

31) Vaněk, Miroslav – Urbášek, Pavel (ed.): *Vítězové? Poražení? Politické elity a disent v období tzv. normalizace. Životopisná interview* (Winners? Losers? The Political Elite and Dissent during Normalization. A Biographical Interview.) Prague, Prostor 2005; Vaněk, Miroslav (ed.): *Mocní bezmocní a bezmocní mocní. Politické elity a disent v období tzv. normalizace. Interpretační studie životopisných interview.* (The Powerful Powerless and the Powerless Powerful. The Political Elite and Dissent during Normalization. Interpretation Studies of Biographical Interviews.) Prague, Prostor 2006.

32) Vaněk, Miroslav (ed.): *Obyčejní lidé...?! Pohled do života tzv. mlčící většiny. Životopisná vyprávění příslušníků dělnických profesí a inteligence.* (Normal People...?! A View of the Life of the So-called Silent Majority. Biographical Narrative of Workers and the Intelligentsia.) Prague, Academia 2009.

even more problematic today than it was several decades ago. This is because they are not "more objective", but also because there will continue to be an increase in the "unsecured" sources among us, e.g. email correspondence.[33] Alexander von Plato suggests that "reduction to merely written documents – and this must be constantly re-emphasized – tends to neglect subjects in a would-be positivist way. Yet there also exists the danger of the other extreme, when, for instance, those working with subjective recollected testimony use these sources without adequate examination."[34] In the view of this prominent German historian, this threat was reduced since plurality was asserted in researching the history of experiences, i.e. the multifacetedness of the employed methods that is often lacking with traditional historians.[35]

Many colleagues/historians have come to believe that this hermeneutic trap can be overcome if the results of quality research are not naively accepted as the "unquestioned truth", but at the same time the testimonies of individuals are not only used as mere illustrations of theses (or of historical speculations) from other sources. Here we might recall our own attempts at "interviews with witnesses" of the late 1960s that in most cases revealed all the aforementioned shortcomings. We thus had to try to find for ourselves the proper use of oral history, and this didn't come until many years later with the help of foreign literature and experiencing first hand all the pitfalls of the new method.

One of the reasons for the criticism of subjectivity and the inaccurate memory of the narrators by some historians undertaking "oral-history research" can be caused by the way these historians conducted their "interviews of experts". I am now referring to projects in which historians examine very specific events and strictly defined themes, meaning that they more "test" their narrators than

---

33) Plato, Alexander von: Zeitzeugen und historische Zunft. Erinnerung, kommunikative Tradierung und kollektives Gedächtnis in der qualitativen Geschichtswissenschaft - ein Problemaufriss. *BIOS* 13, 2000, p. 25
34) Ibid., p. 26.
35) Ibid.

question them.[36] Then, if they encounter weaknesses in the memory's performance, their criticism of subjectivity increases without even examining this subjectivity at all. Not even hours of the "exploitation" of "objects" yields the desired fruit; quite the contrary. The fatigued and often confused narrator is left with the feeling that he or she failed the "test". It is quite obvious that this is a case of a complete misunderstanding of the possibilities of oral history – perhaps even by insufficiently knowledgeable and inexperienced oral historians.[37]

Another theme that interested me in the conducted interviews concerned the future of oral history. The passionate debate at the 14th international IOHA conference in Sydney in 2006 inspired me to ponder this question. The speakers there all emphasized the phenomena of globalization and the digital revolution that distinctly announce their place among the other impulses for the development of oral history. Yet this yields the questions of whether and how oral history is able to accept this new world. Due to new technology, for instance, the way we record, store, catalogue, interpret, share and present oral history communication is changing. What will this development bring?

According to Alistair Thomson, we will soon record all interviews on computers and interview people on the other end of the world. Audiovisual digital recordings will be immediately available in their entirety, and new artificial intelligence will enable everyone to make new and creative connections "within" the borders and "across" the borders of oral history files in using sound, image and text.[38] Michael

---

36) We therefore, fortunately, conceived our first oral history project, completed with the publication of *Sto studentských revolucí* (Vaněk, Miroslav – Otáhal, Milan: *Sto studentských revolucí.* (A Hundred Student Revolutions.) Prague, Nakladatelství lidových novin 1999) as an autobiographical narrative of the entire lives of the narrators up to that point (at that time their twenties and thirties), which culminated with the events of the 1989 Velvet Revolution. These events were incorporated into the narrators' entire lives so that the narrator's memory was equally distributed and at no point in the narration did they feel tested or assessed in either the strength of their memory or in their attitudes.

37) Plato, Alexander von: Zeitzeugen und historische Zunft. Erinnerung, kommunikative Tradierung und kollektives Gedächtnis in der qualitativen Geschichtswissenschaft – ein Problemaufriss. *BIOS* 13, 2000, p. 27

38) Thomson, Alistair: Four Paradigm Transformations in Oral History. *Oral History Review* (USA) 34 (1), 2007, pp. 49–70.

Frisch predicts in this regard that the digitizing of image and sound and its perception via hearing will represent a challenge to the hitherto dominant transcription, i.e. perception via seeing.[39] Paradoxically, the enormous amount of collected material that nobody will be able to interpret can pose a threat to oral history (whereas, in our view, it is the interpretation that is the most important part of oral history). This amassed material will also be very easy to manipulate, since it will have been acquired by people from a wide range of professional levels, without knowledge of the principles of oral history methods and, above all, without observing ethical principles (e.g. politically and ideologically biased material).[40] The threat resides mainly in the fact that such material no longer has to aim for the individual's subjectivity and that it will no longer possess the validity of sociological samples processed using the standard methods. William Moos had pointed this out as far back as 1974.[41] So the conflict of interests of new digital technologies and of the ethical requirements and criteria for working with witnesses set by oral history can lead to a deeper and graver conflict than the disputes between supporters of oral history and its sceptics.

Although some, such as Elizabeth Millwood, feel we should not have even begun to digitize, many oral historians welcome the

---

39) Frisch, Michael: A Shared Authority. Essays on the Draft and Meaning of Oral and Public History. New York, State University of New York Press 1990, p. 188.

40) The role of the media and of its oral history output, of radio or television programs (incidentally showing high audience rates) is quite often mentioned in this discussion. Unfortunately, in our cultural and social milieu (that of the former "Eastern Europe") we come across, in addition to increasingly successful projects, also less successful projects, in which the results are a far cry from the truly scientifically led projects of oral history and, of even greater consequence, work to damage the method that they themselves refer to. These are often manipulative programs without an in-depth understanding of the theme and possessing a political or activistic taint. In many cases this is simply a quest for sensationalism and the ensuing product then violates the basic ethical standards of oral history (relation to the narrator as one who gives), as found, for instance, in the code of ethics of the IOHA or International Anthropological Association. The complicated and very thin line separating the actual presentation of oral history results in the media and the attempt at all cost for the largest possible audience was also pointed out. Many colleagues at international conferences and workshops, especially those from countries west of us, have demonstrated in samples from radio and television programs that even this kind of presentation is possible and desirable.

41) Moss, W. William: The Future of Oral History. *Oral History Review* 3, 1975, pp. 11–15.

possibilities of digital technology or at least accept it, even if with "ambivalent feelings". Ronald Grele approaches this issue too with his typical broadmindedness, drawing attention to what is and will be important for oral history: "[A] good deal of discussions that have gone on here, theoretical discussions, have been discussions about how to deal with the new technology, what the meaning of the new technology is. [...] One of the things about the old Oral History Association was that it had a fetish with how to process things. [...] But the issues were historiographical. *The issues are history* [author's emphasis]. We may be moving into a new technological age but the question is still a historical question."[42]

Even those of us who began to work with oral history (from the moment in which the only bars that threatened us were those of our ignorance) had to clash with conservative historians (as previously mentioned) who doubted the "reliability" and "validity" of oral history. We now face the danger of becoming, in the next fifteen or twenty years, the "conservatives": Will we be convinced that the latest technology can assist in an interview (and at the same time not disrupt it), but that no technology can replace the specific quality of a conversation between two people? Between the interviewer and the narrator, who sit at one table, in one room and experience real, if not time-limited, human contact and not that which is virtual. I don't know how interviewers and narrators in the next generation will feel about the interview "over the Internet". I don't know how this shift toward virtuality will correspond to our current principle – to gain and not betray the narrator's trust. I don't even know if it is possible for modern technology and virtualization of the interview (as in a computer game) to be used to open up the narrator to a virtual interviewer, whose human presence might have caused some inhibition, timidity or embarrassment to arise in the narrator.

While David Dunaway insists that the future of oral history "is here", his colleague Rina Benmayor mainly sees the future in the multidisciplinarity of the field. It is interesting that the topic is no

42) Archive of the Oral History Center of the Institute of Contemporary History. Interviews collection. Interview with Ronald Grele recorded by Miroslav Vaněk, Oakland, USA, October 2007.

longer the method, but the particular field, which points to a major shift in the development of oral history, with all the consequences arising from it. In our view, this is a discussion that still awaits oral history (even views of our narrators show differences in their understanding of terms such as method, discipline, movement and field) and for which this study, given its objective, does not intend to act as a substitute. I therefore will only add my own subjective opinion in the form of a comparison: Is surgery a field within the broader field of medicine, or is it a method that resolves certain health problems in the most effective (most radical, most recent, or even most obsolete) way? Putting it differently, if I imagine a field of study, I see a large, complexly constructed building; if I imagine a method, I see the corridors, stairways and elevators that allow me to move around in this building. Without them a building would be hardly more than a warehouse composed of stones, bricks and panels. If history (and other related humanities) is to hold meaning for life in that it unveils and interprets the ancient or more recent past, it can sometimes (and perhaps must) dare to construct a kind of secret chamber that no stairways lead to, or to build a never-ending corridor. For even life possesses a piece of sci-fi and imagination. Yet, above all, oral history must correspond to real life in its foundations, walls, stairways and roof.

Oral history can be a method applicable in a number of fields and be a field that, through the many increasingly varied methods and technologies, attempts to understand a person and the groups that the individual creates within his closer and broader circles. But we already view oral history as a field, or as a method, and do not have to worry about its future. The words of former IOHA president Rina Benmayor are encouraging in this regard: "I can say that there is a voice here whether you want to recognize it or not. But, I also work with populations and most of my work has been with Latinos. And that is a history that, up until recently, was not in the history books, you know. It was erased, it was ignored. If the traditional historian wanted to gather a history of a group of people that hasn't been documented before they have to go to oral history. There is no other way. And I am seeing now, for example, in proposals and things that come across my desk of students who are getting their PhDs, history students, they are all using oral sources. Give it another ten years, fifteen years I think we are going to be seeing a very strong turn around, at least in some fields of history, social history, and cultural history. I don't know about intellectual history. I think that the young people are coming up, and I saw a lot of them at this conference, are coming up with different agendas and different mindsets about disciplines, and the importance of crossing over disciplines. The new President of the Harvard University, a woman, the first thing she said last year about undergraduate education at Harvard is that we need to become inter-disciplinary. So once that starts to, you know, loosen up a little bit I think there's a place for oral history because I see oral history as a field not just a method. It is a field of study that is multi-disciplinary and inter-disciplinary."[43]

Even Charles Morrissey ponders the future; the past shows, in his words, how important a path oral history has come down. He therefore takes an optimistic view of oral history's future, or the possibility (and necessity) to use it, and believes that oral history will continue to develop. The theme relates to the context of historiography in the United States and points out that oral history is gaining in importance in connection with the growing amount of classified information: "A lot of lawyers in the USA are saying to their clients, 'Put nothing in writing and throw away what you got.' So, what does that leave the future historian, but letters that might read, 'As we discussed on the telephone, please pursue the strategy we agreed on.' What does that really tell you? Well, it doesn't tell you much unless you go to the people who had the telephone conversation, and what was it that you agreed to?"[44] At the same time, however, he points out that the development of oral history can be negatively influenced by the available sources, which is probably a problem

---

43) Archive of the Oral History Center of the Institute of Contemporary History. Interviews collection. Interview with Rina Benmayor recorded by Miroslav Vaněk, Oakland, USA, October 2007.

44) Archive of the Oral History Center of the Institute of Contemporary History. Interviews collection. Interview with Charles T. Morrissey recorded by Miroslav Vaněk, Oakland, USA, October 2007.

that all historians (and not only they) will encounter: "[T]he public funding in this country for what I would call 'humanistic activities', like historical research and explanation, is constantly decreasing. So you have to wonder, the basic financial question, where is the money going to come from to afford all this? And I think that's one of the big differences I've seen in my career, which is now forty-some years, the rise of the presidential library's many foundations, philanthropic foundations, being interested in preserving history as a cultural activity. I don't see as much of that now, and I'll probably see less of that in the immediate future, and that's very regrettable."[45]

The final discussed point and, it should be noted, a specific thematic area, was my request for the narrators to express what route they hope Czech oral historians and Czech Oral History Association would take and what mistakes they should avoid. The respondents' reactions were often awkward in modestly stating that they wouldn't dare advise the Czech association, that perhaps they would be willing to describe what happened in their own country, what the purpose of oral history research was, etc. I therefore decided in this part of the text to provide greater space to direct quotations from the recorded interviews, so that the wishes of prominent members of our oral history community would seem as authentic as possible.

Robert Perks praised the establishment of the Czech Oral History Association, as did other oral historians. Most of them chiefly emphasized the positive impact of our association's activities with regard to the possible interdisciplinary dialogue. Rina Benmayor reacted enthusiastically and spontaneously to the creation of the Czech Oral History Association: "I was thrilled. I have been active in the International Oral History Association and I was thrilled to see that you organized into an Oral History Association. It was wonderful. [...] The only message is to be enthusiastic about it and don't let people tell you that you can't do it."[46] As for her recommendation for Czech oral historians, after briefly considering it she said: "You've

---

45) Ibid.
46) Archive of the Oral History Center of the Institute of Contemporary History. Interviews collection. Interview with Rina Benmayor recorded by Miroslav Vaněk, Oakland, USA, October 2007.

got a huge amount of history to deal with in your country, and I think this is one of the best ways of dealing with it. To generate the democratic opportunity for people to speak, basically, because that is what oral history is. It is democratic at the core. Also not restricting that to any one discipline. Having people from many different disciplines come to your association and embracing that. Look at how psychologists look at memory. Look at how literary people analyze memory. Look at how folklorists deal with memory. Really make it a broader base than just the field of history."[47]

Charles Morrissey first reacted to my final question with a grin, quickly replaced by an expression of concentration. This was due to his attempt to share with less experienced colleagues his advice and recommendations so that it did not sound too "professor-like" coming from one of the legends in the field, but also so that his opinions managed to get through to novice oral historians in the Czech Republic. He then said he had two pieces of advice for us: "[O]ne is, look for those gaps in your national history for which there is little, if any, documentation, and say, 'I will find people who lived that experience and interview them to fill that gap.' And the second one, if you're teaching students of all ages, is enjoy the pleasure. Enjoy the pleasure of not just meeting people, talking with them, making a record of their lives, that has usefulness, not only for their own families, but for their communities, their country, whatever. And also bear in mind that human nature is such, every interview is unique."[48]

Donald Ritchie tellingly described his relationship to oral history and his words could also be taken as a kind of recommendation for oral historians: "We have ethical standards. We have technological standards. These are suggestions about how to do oral history. But the fact of the matter is that there is no one way to do it. You should try to hit the highest standards but in some cases you're going to have to be creative. You're going to have to break the rules and do whatever works in that particular circumstance because that's the only way

---

47) Ibid.
48) Archive of the Oral History Center of the Institute of Contemporary History. Interviews collection. Interview with Charles T. Morrissey recorded by Miroslav Vaněk, Oakland, USA, October 2007.

you are going to get that interview, depending on the interviewee's decisions or whatever the other circumstances are. There are a lot of compromises that go into doing oral history. My recommendation is to do what works for you. [...] *The most important thing is to do it.* [author's emphasis] [...] The greatest thing about doing oral history is actually sitting down with the individual and learning about that individual, having them tell you things that they would never have told anybody else, and getting them to explain their own past and their own events. It is just a wonderful human relationship. I have met the most interesting people over the years. [...] I have learned an enormous amount from them. As a historian I have gained a lot in terms of my own writing from the people that I've interviewed. I feel privileged to be able to record and preserve their interviews."[49]

In Guadalajara, the "outgoing" president of the IOHA, Alistair Thomson, was willing to answer my question regarding recommendations for the Czech Oral History Association. In contrast to the above-cited historians, however, he chose a completely different perspective on this theme (in which he referred to the decision in Guadalajara that the following IOHA conference would be held in Prague): "You are running the conference in Prague and the reason lots of us will come to Prague is to learn from your experience and learn about doing oral history in post-communist Eastern Bloc countries and what have been the challenges and opportunities and innovative things that you do. One of the reasons the international movement of oral history is so exciting is because you learn from difference and different parts of the world. We also appreciate similarities and the two things together are very exciting."[50]

---

49) Archive of the Oral History Center of the Institute of Contemporary History. Interviews collection. Interview with Donald A. Ritchie recorded by Miroslav Vaněk, Oakland, USA, October 2007.
50) Archive of the Oral History Center of the Institute of Contemporary History. Interviews collection. Interview with Alistair Thomson recorded by Miroslav Vaněk, Guadalajara, Mexico, September 2008.

## HOW DID THE INTERVIEWS CONTINUE?

In editing the English version of the publication, I decided to pose two more questions to those interviewed. From the abundance of themes that is currently being dealt with in oral history, I eventually chose two questions that, though in different ways, reflect the problem of understanding history and presenting it in a public space. The first question, inspired by Michael Frisch's concept of shared authority, is devoted to the theme of narrators' participation (of witnesses in general) in the final results of oral history projects.[51] The second question relates to the presentation of historical research and focuses on the coexistence of oral historians, on the one hand, and journalists on the other (here I largely projected my own specific experiences with the work of unprofessional journalists and documentarians).[52]

Simply put, the concept of shared authority provides a new view of the possibilities of interpreting historic events (whether this concerns "great" history, lesser everyday events or personal micro-history). The fact is that, on the one hand, the professional historic public has the power, but also the responsibility to share its knowledge, and, on the other hand, the "lay" public, the very participants in the events, joins in the interpretation and communication of the knowledge. Not only does this contribute to the democratization of history; it also conveys a view of historic events from a new point of view – through the eyes of the participants themselves. Such an approach enriches our understanding and offers new, sometimes even controversial interpretations. The lingering question concerns the manner and the degree of this participation of "ordinary" people

51) In reference to Michael Frisch's concept of "shared authority". The exact wording of the question was: According to you, to what extent is it possible/recommendable to share a narrator's story, as is discussed for example in Michael Frisch's "Shared Authority"? (Frisch, Michael: *A Shared Authority: Essays on the Craft and Meaning of Oral and Public History*. New York, SUNY Press 1990.)

52) The exact wording of the question was: How does oral history co-exist in the environment of journalists who refer to themselves as documentary-makers (in the case their work is considered oral history) and the academic environment? I am asking this because some Czech so-called documentary-makers don't bother with historical accuracy or with ethics towards the narrators. Was or is this similar in your country?

in research projects prepared by a professional historian bound to the methodological and ethical principles of his discipline. It is due to a certain ambiguity in the concept of "shared authority" that I asked the leading figures in the field of oral history to give their views on the given matter.

Rina Benmayor, for instance, spoke in this regard of two "specialists" jointly producing the story – on the one hand, the narrator as the specialist in the experience that he or she shares; on the other hand, the specialist-historian, who oversees the presentation of the story to the public. She feels that this process must always entail mutual cooperation, help, knowledge sharing and a dialogue in which the one side respects the other. David Dunaway also emphasizes the dual nature of creating an oral history interview (and of the ensuing story that is thus constructed). He suggests that an oral history interview is necessarily a product of a certain "negotiation" between the interviewer and the narrator; whether it concerns the story's time sequence, its "veracity" or the analytical framework, in which the story is interpreted.

The theme of joint authorship also appears in Robert Perks's response, in which he suggests that the relationship between the historian, on the one hand, and the respondents, on the other, is an integral part of our final understanding of that which narrators communicate to us. Perks adds that during the interpretation process we can come into conflict with the narrators, i.e. with their interpretations and their vision of the past. He therefore emphasizes that the narrator provides informed consent in which the conditions of the interview itself are defined, as well as specifications of what will happen with the recording and provided information after the interview.

I found Ronald Grele's response to be very helpful in this respect, particularly his mention that sometimes in discussions and texts on the interpretive authority of narrators, the theme of the authority of researchers and historians was sometimes overshadowed. Grele then says that the mutual recognition of the different viewpoints between the researchers and narrators can be very complicated. Yet mutual recognition of our differences is highly important here, "our recognition that the people we talk to have their own ways of interpreting their pasts and have the right to do so in whatever manner they are accustomed to do or the right to know what they know. But, equally, they just understand that we are struggling to know the world and we are not obliged to view the world as they would, that we have a different kind of knowledge of the past."[53] He also finds one of the possible ways to achieve this mutual recognition and understanding: "We will, of course, never fully understand that story as they understand it having lived it but it now strikes me as I write this out that they might understand our understanding as they examine the products we produce: books, articles, films, videos etc."[54]

It is clear from the above, and I lean toward this position, that the mutual recognition of researchers by narrators, and vice-versa, does not have to occur when interpreting interviews. Does that then mean that we have to accept all corrections and changes that narrators bring to the interpretation? Or should we end the possible dispute and disagreement by assuming the stance that if the narrators do not respect our views, we will not respect theirs? Who is the final "authority" in such a case? This is why the informed consent signed by the narrator is such an important part of the interview – it helps solve these kinds of problems and gives us the opportunity to work with interviews in the ways required by rules of the scientific discipline. Alessandro Portelli sees things in a similar spirit and expresses the belief that a narrated story is something that we receive from narrators, something that they share with us. He adds that we should make sure that narrators are aware how the results of the interview are to be worked with (Portelli actually describes the practice of informed consent in his own words). Portelli goes a little further in his research work and even tries to report back to narrators on how their testimony will be quoted in articles, publications, etc. He allows them to actively comment on interpretations, accepts their corrections and tries to negotiate a consensus if he believes the proposed changes diminish the interpretive text. Yet he does not say what is done in the event that an agreement is not reached.

---

53) Excerpt from Grele's email delivered to Miroslav Vaněk on October 17, 2012.
54) Ibid.

Alexander Freund comes up with a more specific contribution to the discussion on shared authority, mentioning one of his projects and very positively assessing the involvement of narrators in the researcher's entire project. He also suggests that not only authority, power and the responsibility to impart to the other one's own knowledge and experiences are shared, but the ownership of the research results are also shared. He points out that cooperation between narrators and researchers requires not only a lot of time, but also patience and mutual trust. Alistair Thomson also mentions a specific research project of his in relation to this and suggests that we do not only offer narrators the chance to tell the story of their lives, but also the chance to become part of history. This is one of the reasons why, in Thomson's view, shared authority has its place in oral history projects. In conclusion, Thomson takes up a topic that I have already mentioned here: the possibility that, in applying the concept of shared authority, we can come into conflict between the responsibilities that we have toward narrators and the responsibility toward historical knowledge.

I was very pleased that I would not have to conclude the imaginary discussion on the theme of shared authority with the idea that there was nearly complete agreement among those asked to give their views on shared authority. Paul Thompson says, and I completely agree, that as a researcher he has a responsibility towards those providing oral history interviews and that this responsibility stems from the ethical rules of oral history. He allows the possibility that he can discuss with some (but not most) the interpretations of their interviews and that in some cases (e.g. academics) the narrators even expect it. Yet he also adds, that he does not think that "most people would want such sharing imposed on them; it's generous of them to agree to be interviewed and we shouldn't try to push them into being quasi-academics."[55]

As previously stated in the second question posed to narrators via email, I reflected upon the current practice (I'm speaking now of the

---

55) Archive of the Oral History Center of the Institute of Contemporary History. Interviews collection. Interview with Paul Thompson recorded by Miroslav Vaněk, London, Great Britain, March 2008.

Czech Republic) in which we encounter the work of some journalists, who do not respect the accuracy of historical data or ethics in relation to their narrators, those providing them with information. In this context, David Dunaway reflects upon the differences in both disciplines – their objectives, audience or work conditions, etc. To a certain extent, he then finds justification for possible historical inaccuracies in that the journalist is always forced to give priority to the story, to the dramatic plot. Ultimately, the media impresses this upon us everyday with its brief reports, illustrated by an abundance of dramatic details. Alexander Freund approaches this matter in a very similar way; he too points out the fact that journalists are increasingly "pressured" into producing work that conforms and satisfies the "market's demands". Charles Morrissey weighed in on the issue by drawing attention to the differences of demands placed on historians, on the one hand, and journalists on the other. In short, most of the other responding oral history specialists also reached similar conclusions.

An inspiring comment in this context came from Ronald Grele, who, within this discussion, extends the concept of the "historian" to the broader population and draws from it certain conclusions concerning the "historiographic" work of journalists: "History is one of the most democratic of disciplines. Almost everyone can become a historian. So, let us admit that when we talk about journalistic documentarians we are talking about people who seek to come to some understanding of the past and present that understanding to a broad public. So, I think my easy answer to your question is that we should treat that product as we would treat any attempt to interpret the past, bringing to bear what we know as historians, what the discourse has been and is currently."[56] Seen purely from the perspective of the plurality of historical events, Ronald Grele is certainly right. Yet the entire matter is much more complicated if we take into account just how large an audience journalists reach everyday; how many individuals they affect in influencing them and forming their opinions.

56) Archive of the Oral History Center of the Institute of Contemporary History. Interviews collection. Interview with Ronald Grele recorded by Miroslav Vaněk, Oakland, USA, October 2007.

In analyzing the responses given by the oral historians, I also appreciated that they all sought a solution that would help deepen the cooperation between the two groups, i.e. would remove some of the problems that arise such as the aforementioned (dis)regard for historical facts. Rina Benmayor and Robert Perks spoke in greatest detail on this matter and certainly would welcome a scenario in which journalists (starting when they are journalism students) became familiar with the methodological, technical and legal aspects of using oral history methods, and adopted them.

I must admit that I was surprised that my expert respondents did not address the ethical aspect of the matter – that journalists often disregarded rules of the ethics when working with people (their sources of information). In their responses, the interviewed oral historians often reacted predominantly to the topic of historical inaccuracies committed by journalists working with life stories. Only Paul Thompson explicitly mentioned the problem of journalists' unethical conduct, which often even breaks the law. Does this mean that the situation in the West is different than in our country? That the journalists there act much more professionally?

I would have to pose this question to my narrators and perhaps create another book of oral history interviews with them. Since, however, this cannot be done "here and now", I will offer here my thoughts on current situations regarding the ethics of historical research in the Czech Republic, which is, according to many of our colleagues, similar in other former Eastern Bloc countries.[57]

So much then for the origination of interviews and their "on-line" continuation. I would now like to invite readers to acquaint themselves with the ideas and views of prominent oral historians.

---

57) My personal experience at a number of conferences and workshops has convinced me that the situation in our region is similar. The oral history panel as part of the ESSHC in Glasgow in 2012 or the Memory between History and Contemporary Politics in East Central Europe workshop in January 2013 in Aarhus randomly come to mind.

# 3/ A book of interviews

## RINA BENMAYOR

"Story is basic, you know. Whether it's a history or a folk story, it's story. And people need stories."

 Rina Benmayor is Professor of Oral History, Literature, and Latina/o Studies at California State University, Monterey Bay. She is the Past President of the Oral History Association in the United States, and has served as President of the International Oral History Association. Her areas of research include oral history and life story; narrative and identity; and digital story-telling. She is co-author of *Migration and Identity* (Transaction Books, 2005), co-editor with William Flores and co-author of *Latino Cultural Citizenship* (Beacon Press, 1997), co-author of *Telling to Live: Latina Feminist Testimonios* (Duke U Press, 2001). She has written various essays on digital storytelling and oral history articles on Puerto Rican women and migration, and first generation Latino college students.[58]

## Interview with Rina Benmayor[59]

**M.V.: I was hoping we could have a small talk which would be very inspirational for me and my colleagues.**

R. B.: First of all let me say that I am honored that you asked me to do this.

---

58) Information based on: Academic Commons [online] [2012-12-22]. <http://www.academiccommons.org/user/rina-benmayor-csumb-edu>.
59) Interview with Rina Benmayor (R. B.) recorded by Miroslav Vaněk (M. V.), Oakland, USA, October 25, 2007.

**M. V.: When was the moment you realized that oral history was for you?**

R. B.: Well I have to back up and tell you that I did my doctoral work in Spanish literature. I didn't know about oral history then, and I am not a historian. When I did my doctoral work, I did a field collection of ballads in oral tradition. Kind of like a folklore project, in my own community. It was a collection of old Spanish ballads retained, preserved and transmitted by Spanish Jews over five hundred years. So I loved the idea, and I went around with my tape recorder to all these older people that came from Turkey and Greece and I asked them to sing for me the old songs that they remembered from their parents and grandparents. Nobody ever told me that I should collect their life stories. So it was definitely a missed opportunity. But I realized that I really enjoyed speaking with people, doing that kind of ethnographic work, interviewing. When I was already teaching I had an opportunity to take a job in New York at a research center called the Center for Puerto Rican Studies, part of the City University of New York. They wanted somebody to develop oral history projects in the Puerto Rican community in New York. So I applied for the job and they gave it to me. I didn't know anything about oral history and neither did they. But it just so happened that it was at the exact the same time, the very same year and almost the very same month that Ron Grele arrived at Columbia. And somebody, a friend of mine from San Francisco told me: "Oh, you have to get in touch with Ron Grele." She knew him from political work. She said: "Oh, you have to get in touch with him. He's now at Columbia." So I got in touch with Ron and it turns out he was an oral historian. Ron was wonderful at that time because he began to bring together all these people from around the world, from Europe and Latin America. He had seminars, and I lived in New York so I could go to the seminars. I became very friendly with other people in New York doing oral history, like Jack Tchen in the Chinese-American community. It was at this moment when everything came together and I started to organize oral history projects and do oral histories. Then, being an academic, I wanted not just to collect them, but I wanted to analyze them, interpret them, and theorize them in a larger way. That was my first encounter with oral history. I was lucky.

**M. V.: The second question is about the power of oral history. What is the power of oral history, what is unique about it?**
R. B.: I think many things. I'm very interdisciplinary in my research. I came out of literature but now I teach many other kinds of things. I look at oral history and see the way the oral history movement has developed over time. My first international meeting was in Oxford, that Paul Thompson organized. That was in the mid-1980s, I think, early to mid-1980s. I began to see that it's not just historians that are doing this; it's lots of other people. I came to it from the perspective of analyzing narrative. Just like you analyze literature, this is another kind of text. Of course, it tells you things that are not written down in history books, obviously. But I think there is also a real power in the dynamic of doing the oral history, of bearing witness to someone else's story. Kind of internalizing that story in a way. Trying to take that story to another audience, if you will. And to translate the story in a way. I think that it is also very powerful for the people telling their stories. It can be very therapeutic. It can be honoring. There is a very human element about it. I think the reason is that it's about story. Story is basic, you know. Whether it's a history or a folk story, it's story. And people need stories. We all need stories because that is how we learn. There is no academic discipline in the university called story telling. There ought to be. I think that the power of it is the voice. The transmission of voice and the transmission of the lived experience through that voice. You can't replicate it in any other way. You can't even write it down properly, you almost have to witness it. And so I think that's for me the essence of it. In some of my classes, for example, oftentimes white students say: "Why are we studying this? This is about 'those' people. This is not about us." This never happens in a class about story; when I get my students to start telling their stories to each other differences, go away and people become allies of each other. And solidarity establishes itself in the room. Rather than fighting and, you know, that kind of thing. I think that story is extraordinarily powerful.

**M. V.: We are sometimes attacked by the so-called "conservative historians" saying that oral history is too subjective; memories are too subjective, etc. What do you say to these voices? What is your opinion?**

R. B.: Well, I don't engage too much in that kind of battle. I think that that may be very particular to the field of history. Not being a historian, I haven't really encountered that too much, in terms of opening up spaces. I'm also teaching now at a university that is experimental. It's multi-disciplinary and inter-disciplinary and so there is never a question about that traditional canon. It has never come up. So I steered away from those kinds of arguments but I think that the obvious answer is that many historians, if they are traditional and conservative, only deal with documented sources. Well who produced those sources? You know! There were people who produced them; there were perspectives in the minds of people who wrote those documents. I can do that from literature. I can say that there is a voice here whether you want to recognize it or not. But, I also work with populations and most of my work has been with Latinos. And that is a history that, up until recently, was not in the history books, you know. It was erased, it was ignored. If the traditional historian wanted to gather a history of a group of people that hasn't been documented before they have to go to oral history. There is no other way. And I am seeing now, for example, in proposals and things that come across my desk of students who are getting their PhDs, history students, they are all using oral sources. Give it another ten years, fifteen years, I think we are going to be seeing a very strong turnaround, at least in some fields of history, social history, and cultural history. I don't know about intellectual history. I think that the young people are coming up, and I saw a lot of them at this conference, are coming up with different agendas and different mindsets about disciplines, and the importance of crossing over disciplines. The new President of the Harvard University, a woman, the first thing she said last year about undergraduate education at Harvard is that we need to become inter-disciplinary. So once that starts to, you know, loosen up a little bit I think there's a place for oral history because I see oral history as a field not just a method. It is a field of study that is multi-disciplinary and inter-disciplinary.

**M. V.: Is it not a method, but a field?**
R. B.: I think it's a field now. It used to be just a method but I think now it is very much a field of study. We don't have PhDs in it, a few masters programs, but I think it is a field because it is engaging very centrally the issue of memory.

**M. V.: Which university do you work at?**
R. B.: I am at the California State University, Monterey Bay. It's only ten or twelve years old, it's very new. The newness will wear off and the conservative forces will take over, and then we will move on to something else that is new.

**M. V.: What do you think about the future of oral history? What do you think are the new challenges?**
R. B.: I think there is a lot of new terrain for oral history. I think, for example, within the university, within the academy or institutions, there is teaching. There is a central place for oral history in teaching and I teach oral history classes but I also integrate it into other classes. The reason I say this is that I teach working class students mostly. They are not going to become university professors. They maybe will become high school teachers. They may become community college teachers, I don't know. A lot of them will go into business. They will go into all different walks of life. They are going to go into community organizing, non-profit work. Oral history skills are skills they can apply in absolutely any field. So I think that there is a real opportunity to teach students how to do oral history as opposed to other kinds of interviewing. You know sociology, surveys, we know all about that. Journalists interview in a different way, but oral historians really do in depth interviews and try to understand the perspective of people who are the makers of history. So I think that when you teach students that way, they actually use this in other areas of their lives. I think it is very important, politically, and in all kinds of ways to go through story and learn about other people through their stories, I think is very important,

politically, and in all kinds of ways. I think there is a huge area that needs to be defined. Everybody's saying that "I'm doing oral history." In community arts, in the art world, and any organization that's doing work with community youth, they all say they are doing oral history when they write their grant proposals. They all say: "We have an oral history component, we're going to learn about the people, etc." It is and it isn't oral history. There is a danger that oral history will become to be diluted. For example, at this conference there are people from all different walks of life and different disciplines. I think that it is important, as the field develops, to really define oral history, and there is a danger in defining it. There are some very simple parameters about what oral history is. Not just going out there and sticking a microphone in front of someone and spending ten minutes with them. That is not oral history. On the other hand, it doesn't mean you have to sit down and spend twenty-five hours doing interviews with an individual. I think also that the digital age means that a lot of stuff will get put up on the web and in archives called oral history. Media has one rule, less is more, so compress, compress, compress. That is what happens in documentary films. You see little snippets here, a person saying a two-minute statement, another two-minute statement and you don't really get the richness of exploring memory that way. So I think that as we become more digital and we put more interviews on the web for more people to have access to, it is important to give them access to entire interviews and not just segments. And to enable research in segments but also in the entire context of the interview. I often think, you know, when you buy a DVD of a movie you get all the extra features, like the director's cut. And so the director is kind of narrating his or her story, or what he or she did in this particular scene. I think that we, as oral historians, need to do that. We need to provide our interpretations of the interviews we collect in a sort of "oral historian's cut". And we need to make those available as well as the original material; I think the important thing about oral history is the interpretation. How do you do that? How do we train people to do that? As a field, I think we have a wide-open opportunity to do that. To foreground and to make more visible how we do interpretation of memory and not just leave the memory alone there for someone to

RINA BENMAYOR

take something out of context. I think also the process of oral history is important to have been documented. We come to conferences and people are always saying: "Well, I interviewed five people, or twenty-five people, and this was the place and this was the context." When you have a media format you don't necessarily have that information. As multimedia evolves and it becomes easier for us to share stories, we should also be sharing what we do with those stories and how we generate those stories. The next meeting of the Oral History Association is going to be in Pittsburgh and it is going to be on the digital. What is this digital thing?

**M. V.: I have one last question. Do you have any recommendations or advice for the Czech Oral History Association, something that could be useful for us?**
R. B.: Well, I was thrilled. I have been active in the International Oral History Association and I was thrilled to see that you organized into an Oral History Association. It was wonderful. The work we are doing is really reaching people because one of the objectives of the International is to go to different regions and stimulate oral history work. The only message is to be enthusiastic about it and don't let people tell you that you can't do it. I don't know the context in the Czech Republic at all. You are from the Academy of Sciences, is that conservative?

**M. V.: I am not. (Laughter)**
R. B.: Whether there are restrictions for people to do oral history, I don't know. I'd say that there is so much change in the world right now, there is always change in the world. I have mostly done my oral history work with multicultural communities, communities that are excluded from the record. You've got a huge amount of history to deal with in your country, and I think this is one of the best ways of dealing with it. To generate the democratic opportunity for people to speak, basically, because that is what oral history is. It is democratic at the core. Also not restricting that to any one discipline. Having people from many different disciplines come to your association and embracing that. Look at how psychologists look at memory. Look at

how literary people analyze memory. Look at how folklorists deal with memory. Really make it a broader base than just the field of history. Maybe that's my bias because I'm not a historian. But it's natural that historians would be looking at oral history. And to connect through all these possible venues. To connect across, to come to conferences, to have your own conferences. Bring conferences to you. Which I hope will happen.

**M. V.: I would like to do that.**
R. B.: I think that's going to be wonderful.

**M. V.: We are ready for it.**
R. B.: Yeah. I think it will happen. I guess that's what I would say. I don't feel like I could give a lot of advice. I was somebody who came in and I am not an oral historian by training, but I found my home here. I found that it is a group of people who love people. Nobody in the United States gets tenure on the basis of oral history work. We come together here and we are kind of more casual. We are not looking at each other, asking how theoretical you are. There are a lot of different aspects of oral history that come together. I think the field has a more democratic feel about it.

**M. V.: That's true.**
R. B.: I found a home here and people embraced me. I think that's the way it is.

**M. V.: In your view, to what extent is it possible/recommendable to share a narrator's story, as it is discussed for example in Michael Frisch's "Shared Authority"?[60]**
R. B.: "Shared authority" is a slippery term that can signify various aspects of the oral history/public history process. In the interview context, it is very clear that the narrative is the product of a shared, collaborative, and dialogic process in which two different "experts" produce a narrative together. The narrator is the expert in

---

60) A new question for the English edition of the book. Rina Benmayor's answer delivered via email, January 3, 2013.

RINA BENMAYOR

the experience and the historian is the expert in shepherding the story. However, the term more readily refers to how the narrative is brought to public view and interpretation and who gets to say what a story means. Digital technologies enable multiple interpreters and museum and public history projects experiment with new ways to elicit and generate multiple interpretations of meaning. However, the absence of a "master narrative" by the intellectual expert does not necessarily mean that there is no organizing/selection/editing/presentation process going on. It is often more hidden. Take my own project as an example. I am involved in designing an oral history virtual walking tour of an historic multicultural neighborhood in which the role of the tour guide and master narrative is disrupted. We want to represent the vibrancy of this neighborhood and the thick levels of intercultural interaction that all the narrators refer to and recall. Rather than having a master tour guide giving the "authoritative" interpretation of the neighborhood, we are using intentional strategies of clustering, juxtaposing, overlapping and intersecting the stories – creating multiple narrators instead of one, and opening the space for multiple interpretations from the tour-takers. However, while the master narrative is disrupted, there are still multiple processes of expert selection, editing, and interpretation at work in structuring the experience. There is no way to avoid this. So, while we strive to open the spaces for shared authority, we should also make visible the interpretive strategies (a sort of "director's cut") that underlie and shape every presentation of a narrative.

**M.V.: How does oral history co-exist in the environment of journalists who refer to themselves as documentary-makers (if their work may be considered oral history) and the academic environment? I am asking this because some Czech so-called documentary-makers don't care much about historical accuracy or ethics towards the narrators. Has it been or is it still like this in your country?[61]**

---

61) A new question for the English edition of the book. Rina Benmayor's answer delivered via email, January 3, 2013.

R. B.: I begin my undergraduate oral history class by having them read Mary Kay Quinlan's article in the Oxford Handbook of Oral History on the difference between an in-depth interview and journalistic practice. She is both an oral historian and a journalist and makes very useful distinctions between the interviewing methods. Many of my students want to become journalists and think that the interviewing they will conduct in my class is what they are trained to do in journalism. They undergo a much different training and experience of in-depth interviewing and at the end, are able to understand at an experiential level the differences between the two methods and practices. Not only is the interview structured differently (investigative journalism might come closer to oral history practice), but the ethical guidelines for journalism differ radically from ours. I believe that journalism programs ought to include an oral history training component, to enable a more critical view of their own ethical and disciplinary practice.

## DAVID KING DUNAWAY

"The power of oral history is in its authenticity, in that the people who are making, who are a part of history are representing it, instead of waiting for some historian 40 or 100 years from now to represent history for them. I say that all history involves a leap of imagination based upon serious documentary research."

For the last thirty years David Dunaway has documented the work of Pete Seeger resulting in *How Can I Keep From Singing? The Ballad of Pete Seeger* (McGraw Hill, 1981; revised, updated and republished by Villard/Random House, 2008). Author of nine volumes of history and biography, Dunaway's specialty is the presentation of folklore, literature, and history via broadcasting. He's been active in radio since 1972, but over the last dozen years he has been Executive Producer of award-winning national radio series for Public Radio International, including *Writ-*

*ing the Southwest* (1995), *Aldous Huxley's Brave New Worlds* (1998), *Across the Tracks: A Route 66 Story* (2001), and *Pete Seeger: How Can I Keep From Singing?* (2008). He is currently a DJ for KUNM-FM and a professor at the University of New Mexico in Albuquerque.[62]

### Interview with David King Dunaway[63]

**M. V.: When did you decide to go into oral history? Why do you use it? Do you remember when you figured out it was the thing for you?**

D. D.: I was a graduate student at the [University of California] Berkeley in history and literature (American Studies) and in order to have an antidote to the seminar room I decided that what I really needed was a way to reach out to the public. So I wandered from the seminar rooms at Berkeley down to the local public radio station with the popular community broadcasters and started doing interviews for them. I did that for about six months and then finally went back up to the history department and took a seminar in oral history. About the second seminar meeting from Willa Baum, who is one of the founders of the American oral history movement and also later on the editor of Oral History: An Interdisciplinary Anthology with me, sort of classic work, I stood up in class and said, "I feel like that character in Molière who walks onto the stage and says 'I just realized I've been speaking prose all my life'." And I realized that I had spent years doing oral history without ever understanding the concept of oral history – that there was a discipline, that there was a body of literature. And it was at that point that I decided that my contribution to oral history would be in editing the first anthology of oral history and contributing an article on making documentaries from oral history, because very often oral historians are more concerned with collecting material than returning it to the communities that have created it. It seemed to me that if we only collect oral history and we don't return it, we might in some sense be guilty of cultural theft – taking people's testimonies that they expect will be

62) Information based on: David King Dunaway Website [online] [2012-12-22]. <http://www.davidkdunaway.com/>.
63) Interview with David King Dunaway (D. D.) recorded by Miroslav Vaněk (M. V.), Oakland, USA, October 24, 2007.

available and instead sticking them on a shelf somewhere. A lot of times oral history is not even transcribed. It's put in a little spot and then someone knows about it, it's on a little card somewhere, but the public doesn't have the continuity of history that is so important, and I think that my goal is that someone will hear one of my documentaries and they will say, "Oh, I know better stories than that," and they will then engage in the world of oral history and themselves become oral historians. So my moment, to answer your question, is when I realized that oral history was what I had already been doing.

**M. V.: I would like to know your opinion about the power of oral history. What new aspect could oral history bring to understanding our past and present?**
D. D.: The power of oral history is in its authenticity, in that it offers to the people who are making, who are a part of, are representing it, instead of waiting for some historian 40 or 100 years from now to represent history for them, the possibility that individuals can speak themselves for their own part of history. Here in Oakland today we have been seeing presentations from the Black Panther party, which began five blocks from here. These are the participants in history who are presenting their own history. Now, that doesn't mean we don't need to be uncritical about it – it doesn't mean that we as scientists and researchers don't need to interrogate that record to ask for self-criticism and not just celebration. For me the unique power of oral history is the way it allows those people who have often been written out of the historical record, who have been told that they aren't important, to tell their own stories. And thus it reorients history to make all of us a part of history, not in a passive way, but in an active way, that we too are a part of history. That to me is the power of oral history. It allows us to create testimony on very important things that if the oral historian is doing their job, is thoroughly researched, is thoroughly prompted, thoroughly documented, thoroughly grounded, but basis from someone else's experience and not our perspective. In an oral history interview, the people come from different perspectives. The historian has done some reading, has looked at documents, has a body of theory that they understand and

have considered, and they bring all these things into the moment. The subject or narrator comes from a different perspective. He or she lived through it, so their experience is informed, well, experientially, their testimony is experiential and the historian's is documentary. It's that wonderful meeting of, "Well, this was my experience," and someone else asking them, "Yes that was your experience, but look at this and look at this and look at this, and tell me how you now see that experience, perhaps, differently." So it's a combination of recording eye-witness events with contextualizing those events, and that combination is what makes oral history magical.

**M. V.: What about a quite frequent problem that oral history is too subjective, that memory is very selective. What would you say to these voices?**
D. D.: Here's what I say (and I have been doing this for 35 years, so I've had to say it more than once): I say that all history involves a leap of imagination based upon serious documentary research, and that's as true for conducting an interview as it is for reading a diplomatic letter. The same standards of testing, of contextualizing, of challenging the evidence against the historical record apply to an oral document that applies to a written document. I have suggested in some of my writings that history constructed from oral sources may be different in some ways from history constructed exclusively from written documentary sources. It would take too long to give that lecture here, but let me just point out that the historian, when he comes to oral history becomes a field worker and finds himself sharing the issues involved that folklorists do, that ethnomusicologists do, that anthropologists do, that linguists do, when they work in the field. I think my favorite piece, if I were to sum up, from my writings on this very point, is called "Field Reporting Oral History" from the Oral History Review 1987. It tries to rise in that essay, which I wrote in Denmark as a fellow of the Danish Research Council, it tries to explore what it means for a historian to become a field worker and what sensibilities they must develop if they are going to work with moving targets, and targets that are interactive. History at that point becomes interactive. Your informed documentary reading of

the past meets my experiential one, and together we create, I have also argued, a synthetic moment which is neither in your time nor my time; it is a negotiated past and a negotiated authority. So for your colleagues who have had questions about oral history as a research method need to understand that there is a vast literature on oral historiography, and that it involves a leap of faith in which an individual becomes a field worker and understands what's involved in that and understands that the document created from an oral history interview is a trialog, not a dialog – an historian, a narrator, and it is Cleo, the muse of history, that we all serve. And that these documents can't necessarily be understood in the time of the interview, but have greater profound implications five years from now, ten years from now, forty years from now. That we are not only creating a historical moment but we are creating a historical record. And then I would also point out, finally, because it's my specialty, that a well-reported oral history document has uses far beyond written history. It can become a part of film, it can become part of television, it can become part of museum exhibits, and it can become most suitably a part of radio that can use the palette created from the texture of voices to create a document which is a collage which can bring multiple viewpoints, multiple perspectives into play in a way that the work of a single historian working with a single set of research documents, cannot.

**M. V.: What do you think about the future of oral history, of oral historians?**

D. D.: In the second edition to *Oral History: An Interdisciplinary Anthology*, I tried to take up in the introductory essay, called "The Interdisciplinarity of Oral History", this key, very important question on the future of oral history. To me, the future of oral history has already happened. It has moved from a documentary method into a standard research method applicable to a wide range of disciplines. Initially oral history was conceived of as tape recording source documents that someone way later on would come to. But we have now realized that oral history is both a discipline and a method, and that the method has disciplinary implications and the discipline has

DAVID KING DUNAWAY

methodological ones. To me the greatest achievement of this work *Oral History: An Interdisciplinary Anthology,* first published 23 years ago, is that it has been used by anthropologists, by ethnohistorians – our method, our innocent little method that we originally conceived of sixty years ago when the process began during the New Deal in the United States and in the earliest programs at Columbia University in New York, our innocent little method where we would throw away the tapes once we had the transcripts has become standard in using historical research. I just had a conversation with a professor from the University of Maryland, he tells me that in the history department, 50 % of their dissertations rely on oral sources collections, 50 %. Now perhaps that's not the same yet in the Czech Republic, but it will come – it will come, it's inevitable. It has to come, for a wide variety of reasons, I would suggest. First of all, the use question that we just talked about, because people will get their history more and more from listening to the radio, from the Internet, where we want to hear these voices. They will come from film and documentary procedures for which oral history properly recorded is an excellent source. So the future is here, Professor Vaněk, it's already here, and it's a matter of historians adapting to a new frame of reference and a new set of technologies and a new set of re-instilling historical consciousness to a wider public.

**M. V.: I'm pleased to hear that, it's encouraging. Is there any message you want to send to your Czech oral history colleagues?**
D. D.: First of all, many greetings to them. It's a great thing that you have managed so much in oral history, that you founded the Oral History Centre, the Czech Oral History Association. The world of oral history needs more researchers, doing the in-depth research which reveals holes in the historical record; it needs more interviewers, willing to ask the hard questions based on that research; it needs more transcribers, ready to listen hard for the nuances of historical testimony; and above all, it needs more public programmers who can return the history so gathered to the communities that created and cared for it. My wishes are for all of these to flock to your association and particularly young, dedicated historians who

will work in their community's historical treasure chest and inspire other under-thirties with its golden memories.

**M. V.: In your view to what extent is it possible/recommendable to share a narrator's story, as it is discussed for example in Michael Frisch's "Shared Authority"?[64]**

D. D.: All oral history involves the shared construction and reconstruction of reality. Thus, Frisch's "Shared Authority" was taking a new look at a practice long understood by oral historians. It problematized the issues of the first generation of oral historians, who were concerned about veracity, plausibility, and other issues in eliciting historical fact from eye-witnesses. But the dual nature of the creation of oral history, reflected in its law and custom, theoretically engages every thoughtful oral historian. What time period, for example, is an oral history interview constructed from? The time period of the interviewer, who sits in the present and reflects on the past via existing historical resources? Or is it the time of the incident itself, in which our narrator lived, about which he tries now to recall, and make sense? Inevitably, the time sequence of an oral history interview is negotiated; and so are its degrees of truthfulness, the import of questions asked, and the questioner, and the analytical framework used to understand the testimony generated.

**M. V.: How does oral history co-exist in the environment of journalists who refer to themselves as documentary-makers (if their work may be considered oral history) and the academic environment? I am asking this because some Czech so-called documentary-makers don't care much about historical accuracy or ethics towards the narrators. Has it been or is it still like this in your country?[65]**

D. D.: I've produced documentaries for 30 years based on oral history, and I teach documentary history, theory, and praxis at the university level. I offer this as background to my remarks, which follow, involv-

---

64) A new question for the English edition of the book. David King Dunaway's answer delivered via email, November 17, 2012.
65) A new question for the English edition of the book. David King Dunaway's answer delivered via email, November 17, 2012.

DAVID KING DUNAWAY

ing relationships between documentary-makers and oral historians. For my further musings on this topic, see *Field Reforming Oral History and Radio and the Public Use of History* (Dunaway and Baum, 1984, 1996).

My first point is that documentary workers and oral historians have different outcomes and different audiences for their work. The oral historian is fundamentally interested in generating resources for him or herself and other scholars to analyze. Their audience is usually fellow researchers and writers; though this has been changing. The documentarian is in the business of re-recording, narrating, and re-contextualizing the testimony given. Their audience is a necessarily public one, who expects a finished product. An oral historian's typical audience is presumed to be willing to sift through material.

Their method differs: oral historians return transcripts and conduct extensive research, and presume collaboration. Documentarians often must move too quickly to collaborate, and their research is usually situation and one time-dependent.

The point is that, besides audiences and methodology, the role of story plays out differently in their work. For all historians, story can be an impediment to the actual recollection of an event; the more times the story of an event is told, the less value of its factual recollection. But for the documentarian, the challenge is to discover a dramatic plot in a series of volunteered facts. The facts collected by the oral historian may lack context; they may be so poorly recorded that the documentarian cannot use the audio or video; they may be rich with detail; but, fundamentally, they do not constitute a story for broadcast until a documentarian enters the process and sifts and winnows the truckloads of facts into a dramatically constructed narrative. At times, the pressure to storify for documentarians exceeds the pressure for historical accuracy. Faced with a fact that may or may not be accurate, but which adds spice to the narrative, a documentarian will often be tempted to give greater credibility to an incident which fulfils the need to represent reality in a dramatic fashion.

## ALEXANDER FREUND

"It's not just writing marginalized people into history, but also having them participate in the creation of history. Having them understand what history is – that history is not this one true story of the past, but is a construction in the present that is very politically interested, politically motivated, and is a political act. So I think through oral history people understand that."

 Alexander Freund (M. A., Simon Fraser University 1994, Ph.D., Bremen University 2000) is Professor of history and Chair in German-Canadian Studies at the University of Winnipeg. He is a founding Director and Co-director of the University of Winnipeg's Oral History Centre. He is President of the Canadian Oral History Association and co-editor of the association's journal, *Oral History Forum d'histoire orale*. Recent publications include the edited volume *Beyond the Nation? Immigrants' Local Lives in Transnational Cultures* (University of Toronto Press, 2012), with Pablo Pozzi et al. (eds.), *Oral History Forum d'histoire orale 32* (2012), *Edición Especial/Special Issue Historia Oral en América Latina / Oral History in Latin America*; and with Alistair Thomson (eds.), *Oral History and Photography* (Palgrave, 2011; paperback and Kindle 2012).

### Interview with Alexander Freund[66]

**M. V.: I would like to know if you remember the moment when you encountered oral history, a method that is important for you... Do you see in your professional life a moment when you became conscious of it?**

A. F.: I had a background in journalism when I started university. When I started graduate school at Simon Fraser University in Canada I got into oral history in a more theoretical way, perhaps more than others do. I was looking at a project about German immigrant women in post-World War Two Vancouver. The first fact that I learned about these women was a statistical number – 25,000 single

---

66) Interview with Alexander Freund (A. F.) recorded by Miroslav Vaněk (M. V.), Guadalajara, Mexico, September, 2008.

German women immigrated to Canada during the 1950s to work as domestic servants. I could have done a history of them, based only on archival, written documents. But it seemed natural to go out and interview them and get their stories.

I was also interested in figuring out the theoretical issues of insider–outsider interviewing. I approached them as an insider in a sense, because they were German immigrant women and, as an international student, I was sort of a German immigrant, at least a German in Canada. But I was an outsider because they were women, and I was a man. Then there was the idea that I was an academic, and they were mostly working class, so not from an academic background.

I mostly wanted to explore these ideas, and I mean in the end, eventually gender and class didn't really make too much of a difference. The dominant dynamic in the interview situation ended up to be around age. They considered me a sort of "greenhorn", a newcomer they would teach about living in Canada. I was intrigued, and also after I had done the interviews – trying to make sense of these interviews, trying to figure out what do they mean as sources for historians, how to deal with memory. All of the intellectual challenges of using oral history – this was very appealing to me. I have been doing interviews ever since. I mean there was this idea of getting out and talking to people and hearing their stories. You're not sitting in archive by yourself, you know, it's sort of the social aspect of that. So this is the moment.

**M. V.: Thinking about some of the advantages and disadvantages, do you feel that oral history has its own power that is important for understanding? There are a lot of ideas, but I want to know your opinion.**

A. F.: For me, it works on two levels – one I've already mentioned, is that it is intellectually fascinating to work on oral history as a source, as a text. It really makes you think about history in a way that other sources don't, and in part because oral historians have been, I think have been thinking more critical about sources and oral history sources. So I find it intellectually stimulating. It is also intellectually stimulating because as oral historians, we are not only willing to go out into other disciplines, but we are forced to go into other disciplines, to make sense of oral history. We read also into anthropology, folklore, social sciences and so on.

That is intellectually very stimulating. But oral history is also a way of democratizing history that is very important, and as to what Paul Thompson says, to democratize history on many different levels. You know it's not just writing marginalized people into history, but also having them participate in the creation of history. Having them understand what history is – that history is not this one true story of the past, but is a construction in the present that is very politically interested, politically motivated, and is a political act. So I think through oral history people understand that.

Finally, it democratizes history. Also, it's something that I only experienced recently, as I've been able to teach oral history. It helps students in particular to understand what history is and the power of history and to develop a critical approach to history, especially at the undergraduate levels. When they go out and do the interviews, that's when they begin to understand the complexity of history. That history is not simply what's in the textbook – the stuff you learn by rote memory for the test – it's really about constructing a story that makes sense that helps you in the present. So in those ways, it really democratizes history.

**M. V.: What is your answer to the skeptics saying that memory is subjective, questioning the validity of oral history research?**
A. F.: In Canada there are still many historians who are skeptical, and if they are skeptical, the first thing I would say, or at least I would want to say, maybe I'm not quite as harsh, is: Why don't you go and read up the literature, as with any other field in history? If you were a modern historian, you wouldn't make any sort of casual remarks about medieval studies without some background knowledge. That's sort of what we do, we read up on stuff, then we can develop a critical understanding. If they're skeptical about oral history, and haven't really read in the field, I would tell them to read the chapters on evidence and memory in Paul Thompson's Voice of the Past, then they sort of know where the debate is. Or read Sandro Portelli's Death

of Luigi Trastulli, and then we can talk on that level about memory or subjectivity. Where it's not about forgetting, getting a story right or the dates right, that's not what oral history is about. It's about memories and creating counter memories and counter history. So that would be my major reaction.

And then after they've done that, I would be very interested in talking to them about oral history as a source, or as a text, and compare notes with other sources. That is sort of what is missing from oral history – to look at other kinds of sources that we use for history and see how we can learn from each other. We can certainly learn from oral historians, but there are certain aspects we can learn as well. So I think we need more of that exchange of ideas, of critical approaches to sources, to history in general.

**M. V.: Is oral history a method or a field? Is it important?**
A. F.: Well, I think oral history has different meanings, and it's important to know the different meanings because it makes sense to be precise in the terminology. But it's also important not to be dogmatic about terms. To me personally, I use the term "oral history" to explain that oral history is a source, oral history is a method and oral history is a movement. And these are three different ideas. It is confusing if you are not clear with what you are talking about. So it's useful to be clear what meaning of oral history you're talking about. It's not only a method and certainly, it's a field of literature that is interdisciplinary in that sense. It's certainly a community of people who exchange ideas about oral history – as such, it's certainly a field.

**M. V.: You said movement. What does that mean? That the method is new, the view on history is new?**
A. F.: The movement is about democratizing history. I think it has radical roots. It does come out of the 1960s social history workshop movement – the idea to change history, to rewrite history. And that was a radical move. It was about getting certain people into the history departments, trying to move into positions of power in academia. It was about changing our understanding of history – that it was not

a master narrative, that there were counter memories and counter histories that were just as valuable. So it was about changing our understanding of history, which in popular culture and society in general is still very traditional. I think it has these radical roots. It's got lost a bit, I think, in part because oral history as a movement has branched out and several aims have been achieved. If you look at history departments in North America – they've become much more diverse. So those aims have been achieved.

Of course that generation of the 1960s has moved into positions of power and become established and in some cases less radical. The next generations, at least in Canada, there was an opportunity lost to transfer that memory of the beginnings. So many Canadians don't know about the history of oral history in Canada, or the general international movement. But I think there is an opportunity to revive the more radical roots. I really like what Ron Grele said in Sydney about oral history as a movement to demystify globalization. I think that's a wonderful new aim for the movement – to document how globalization is experienced on the ground. How globalization, capitalism affect people in a negative way, or more generally how globalization changes people's lives, in all kinds of ways. I think it's our role and responsibility, as oral historians, to document that and make sense of that. And certainly oral history also then provides the space, as Al [Alistair Thomson] said, to empower people and to be used as political activism.

I think a lot of people think of oral history as either academic or activist, but I think oral history and history in general is always political. Whatever you do, it's a political intervention, in the social discourse, in the structure of society. Whether you write conservative history, or liberal history, or radical history, it's still political. There's no such thing as neutral history. It is political.

**M. V.: What do you think about the future movement?**
A. F.: My views are limited mostly toward North America, and that is what I see now, especially in the United States. The mushrooming of storytelling on the web, mostly, where people use digital media, to record stories and to put them out on the web. And I'm not quite sure

ALEXANDER FREUND

where that is going, and what the implications are. So, not just Story-Corps – it's all over the place. Well in Germany, at least, if you look at the way television journalists have used eyewitness testimonies, oral history interviews to create documentaries. That is something that I think oral historians, we need to look at more directly, and figure what the meaning and implications of that are.

On the one hand, these huge initiatives, which often have a lot of money. They ignore oral history and all of what we have created, in terms of critical approaches to testimony, to memories. So that's a problem, and I think we need to be more active in making them listen to us. But it's also this sort of this uncritical use of digital media that I find troubling. You can't just go out there to record stories, just because it's so easy now and so cheap now to record them, to record them on video and digital audio. That is something that we have to look at more critically. So I'm ambivalent that oral history is going to a digital age – that's clear. I'm ambivalent about the opportunities and dangers. It's both; I think we need to reflect more about the dangers.

**M. V.: Do you have any recommendations about oral history for students?**

A. F.: I'll tell you very briefly what happened in Canada. In Canada, the oral history movement started in the early 1970s, and it was led by archivists, who were in institutions. They got quite a bit of funding from the national and provincial archives to set up conferences and publish a journal, and so on. That was all fine, until the end of the 1980s, that's when drastic budget cuts to archives made it basically impossible for archivists to continue in this role. But in the process of institutionalizing, or organizing oral history in Canada, they had not made alliances with other people. Journalists and academics often left the association in the 1980s. At the end of the 1980s, the Oral History Association almost voted itself out of existence. It was avoided, but it was dead, basically. We've been trying to recover this over the last years, with the help of a few colleagues at my university and elsewhere. But we have been focusing mostly on the association's journal, of which we are very proud. We have made it into an open access online journal that everyone from around the world can access without any costs. It's free of charge. You can read it at www.oralhistoryforum.ca.

The lesson then is, when you create this association of oral historians in the Czech Republic, to make sure you have partners in different sectors of society – not just archivists, not just academic historians, but all over the place. To make sure you have several bases, in case one breaks away, for whatever reason. The other is you want to ensure there are mechanisms to transfer the memory of oral history in the Czech Republic to the next generation. That was also what was missing in Canada. The new generation of oral historians in Canada doesn't know much about the roots of oral history in Canada, and that's a big problem. So if you can find ways to make sure the next generation knows about the history of oral history in the Czech Republic that would be very, very helpful.

**M. V.: In your view, to what extent is it possible/recommendable to share a narrator's story, as it is discussed for example in Michael Frisch's "Shared Authority"?[67]**
A. F.: Over the past two years, I have had the great fortune to receive funding for my first truly collaborative project. From 2011 to 2014, we are working with several refugee communities in Manitoba, Canada to document the history of refugees in Manitoba since 1945. One project recovers oral history interviews done with post-World War Two refugees, then re-interviews these early narrators, and then interviews with their children and grandchildren. We want to find out how memories of state violence, displacement and home are negotiated between different generations.

In the second project, members of the Salvadorian community have participated in several oral history workshops to learn the skills to document their history. They want to pass their stories on to their children, who often know very little of their experiences before and during the bloody civil war of the 1980s or the long, long

---

67) A new question for the English edition of the book. Alexander Freund's answer delivered via email, December 4, 2012.

ALEXANDER FREUND

migrations from El Salvador through Central and North America to finally Winnipeg or other places in Manitoba. For this project, I provide resources, oral history training, and administrative support, but it is the community members, who initially approached me with the idea, who designed the project, developed questions, did the research, conducted interviews, and created presentations and publications. Ownership of the research findings is negotiated and decided collaboratively.

Such collaboration takes a lot of time, patience, and trust – on both sides. But it makes so much sense. Aren't we always surprised, whenever we hear someone's life story, how resourceful people are? At least that's what happens to me. Every time I hear someone's life history, I am simply amazed. So, if our narrators have these resources, let's make use of them in the research process. Let's break down the barrier between researchers and subjects. At every single meeting, the community researchers surprise me. Whether it is that they personally know lots of people in the Salvadorian government, were present at the funeral of Archbishop Óscar Romero after his assassination in 1980, or identify themselves, relatives, or friends in newspapers and history books. It is one thing to read a newspaper article about the Central American Solidarity movement in 1980s Manitoba by yourself, as a historian. It is quite another to read the same article together with a group of people who were leaders in this movement, who know every single person mentioned, and remember the places and events. But the learning is mutual. It is a great feeling to see how much they enjoy piecing together a part of their history with some of the skills you taught them. This is truly mutual learning.

This experience has also deeply influenced and changed my approach to teaching students. I want my students to be just as excited about their research as the members of the Salvadorian community are about their research. That means I had to find ways to make research and learning in the classroom just as collaborative. I now tell my students that they are researchers working on this refugee history project and their work will not end up in a waste basket, but, with permission from all participants, in an archive, a book, or a website. Once I started doing that, students then began to develop their own oral history projects which they pursued for months and months after the courses had finished. So, to answer your question: I believe that collaboration is the most effective way of sharing authority – by extending this sharing to all phases and aspects of oral history projects.

**M. V.: How does oral history co-exist in the environment of journalists who refer to themselves as documentary-makers (if their work may be considered oral history) and the academic environment? I am asking this because some Czech so-called documentary-makers don't care much about historical accuracy or ethics towards the narrators. Has it been or is it still like this in your country?[68]**

A. F.: My short answer is: yes. I think this is a phenomenon, perhaps even a result, of globalizing news media markets. Documentary film makers and even more so journalists work within very difficult, market-driven structures that do not encourage a critical engagement with history, at least not in Canada and Germany, the two countries I know best. The recent crisis in journalism, especially print journalism, has further increased pressures on journalists to conform to "market demands". This is often compounded by conservative governments that play up nationalistic and militaristic national narratives. This is certainly true under the current conservative government in Canada, which has been extremely aggressive in re-writing the national story of Canada from that of Canada as a peacekeeping nation and multi-cultural society to a story that glorifies militarism, Canada's "British heritage", and conservative Christian values. We end up with lots of feel-good stories about veterans' war memories, but they're never asked how killing another person changed them and their own lives.

The question for historians is this: How do we change this (assuming that we can)? How can we help journalists and documentarians to make historically and ethically sound films? I think

---

68) A new question for the English edition of the book. Alexander Freund's answer delivered via email, December 4, 2012.

ALEXANDER FREUND

my previous answer leads to one answer. Among the people we get excited about oral history – and who as a result become more critical of what history is and does – there are future (or perhaps even present) documentary makers and journalists. The reiteration rather than critiquing of nationalist narratives in films is generally not the fault of the documentary makers or journalists – they often start out with great idealism and are among our brightest students before beginning their media careers – but of international media corporations that privilege advertising revenue over solid reporting. Oral historians have all the tools we need to support documentary film makers and journalists in their endeavors to produce films we would endorse. But I think this is hard work that functions only at the local level, through networking, contacts, teaching through public workshops, and so on. Some of my colleagues have done this with great success, but let us also not forget at what cost: the time they spent working with documentary film makers was time they did not spend writing articles and books. Collaboration is a painstaking but important process, but under the pressure to publish, we can often engage in this only after we have received tenure and promotion. Throughout our careers as academics, however, it is important that rather than brushing journalists off as uncritical amateurs, we engage them in the same way we do our students and narrators. Let's not forgot that journalists and film makers have great resources, not just in technical skills and contacts, but also in their understanding of how to tell stories visually. If we find ways to collaborate and learn from each other, both sides will benefit.

## RONALD GRELE

"What we are asking people to do in the oral history interview is to become historians, to put together in some semblance of a rational discourse the various events of their lives, explain them, put them in that context, and to tell us how the past has emerged, how changes have occurred. We are asking them to become historians, and what we're really tapping into is historical consciousness."

Ronald Grele is the former Director of the Columbia University Oral History Research Office. Prior to coming to Columbia he directed the Oral History Program at the University of Carolina, Los Angeles and served as Research Director at the New Jersey Historical Commission and Assistant Director of the Ford Foundation Oral History Project. He began his career in oral history as an interviewer and archivist at the John F. Kennedy Oral History Project. He has been awarded a Fulbright teaching appointment at the University of Indonesia and has conducted workshops and seminars on oral history throughout Europe, Asia, and Latin America. In 1988 he was elected President of the Oral History Association and was for a number of years editor of The International Journal of Oral History.

He is the author of *Envelopes of Sound: The Art of Oral History* among other works, and editor of *Subjectivity and Multiculturalism in Oral History.* He received his doctorate from Rutgers University and has taught at Lafayette College, The California State University at Long Beach and Kingsborough Community College. He has served as a consultant on number of oral history projects and for a number of museums and historical agencies. He has undertaken projects on the history of the Garrett Corporation in Los Angeles, McKinsey & Company, and the Boston Consulting Group. He has conducted interviews for the Columbia Oral History Office with women graduates of the Columbia Law School and with directors and officers of The Atlantic Philanthropies and the General Atlantic Group, and for a community history project documenting the social and cultural history of Harlem. He is currently conducting interviews for the Rule of Law Project and the Carnegie Corporation Project.

### Interview with Ronald Grele[69]

**M. V.: I would like to ask a couple of questions which could be very important. The first is about when you came across oral history, what was the decisive moment when you knew it was for you?**

R. G.: There are two parts to that. The first job in oral history I ever had... I got that job because I was looking for a job and I went to work for the Kennedy Library in the summer of 1965 and I worked there for a year with Charlie Morrison. He was my boss at the time, that was my first job out at the Kennedy Library, and I did not find it a very exciting job for any number of reasons. There were scholarly reasons; they did not give us access to the Kennedy papers. So we were doing the interviews just based on news reportage. It was during the Vietnam War, the Vietnam War was heating up, and I really disliked working for the government. My wife and I lived in Washington, we did not like working in Washington, DC. We wanted to get away from the east coast, so that job came to an end. A number of years later I hooked up again with Charlie Morrison who was doing a project on the Ford Foundation. He had received a contract to do oral history for the Ford Foundation and for a number of complicated reasons I ended up as the assistant director on that project. And it was on the Ford Foundation that I actually began to take what I was doing as an oral historian seriously. The way in which we divided that work was that Charlie did most of the interviews and I did most of the inside work, the processing of the interviews. In those days what that meant was that we did something called audit editing, which meant I listened to the tape and looked at the transcript to make sure the transcriber had done it correctly. First of all, I would listen to the tapes to make notes for the transcriber. Then I would listen to the tape and read the transcript again to make sure she had done it, then it would go back to the person who had

---

69) Interview with Ronald Grele (R. G.) recorded by Miroslav Vaněk (M. V.), Oakland, USA, October, 2007.

been interviewed, that person would send you their corrections and I would have to look at it again. So each interview I listened to it twice, read the transcript three times. So gradually, as I listened to those interviews, something more than just the search for facts was happening. That we were interviewing people who had a distinct world view... These were people who were giving away money at the Ford Foundation and they were in a sense planning the world, they were deciding what part of the social sciences in the United States and internationally would be funded, which wouldn't be funded, they were making decisions as to the nature of educational systems in Nigeria, they were making decisions as to who in Indonesia would get what kinds of money for what kinds of... it was quite clear that this was the American establishment giving out its money. And behind that was a view of the world in which history was very important.

This was still the cold war period, and it was an insight into the ideology of American liberalism. At the same time as this was going on for reasons that were quite independent, and we could get into that in a longer interview, I was doing a lot of reading in French Marxism and structuralism, French Marxism and Louis Althusser for certain kinds of political reasons. The structuralism simply because I was very attracted to finding out some way of handling the massive amount of data and I was very affected by a folklorist by the name of Henry Glassey who was a structuralist and had some wonderful, wonderful work. And so at the same time as I was reading Lévi-Strauss and Chomsky and Lacan and I became very interested in the question of ideology and figuring out what is an ideology and then applying it directly to the interviews. I was using what is the ideology here. It was not Althusser's various claims to scientific certitude in Marx that was so important to me but rather his discussion of ideology which I touched upon in the interview, and, most importantly his methodological commitment to what he called "symptomatic reading". It is that set of ideas that inform my work at that time, how can we read a text in order to discover the hidden levels of discourse from which it emerges, and account not only for what was said but for what was left unsaid, what is the significance of the questions

RONALD GRELE

that were asked and what is the significance of those which were not. I still find those issues key to our work in uncovering the ways in which people (regardless of any formal training in history) make their own history, or more correctly live their own history.

And so I began to think about how history is made, that what we are asking people to do in the oral history interview is to become historians, to put together in some semblance of a rational discourse the various events of their lives, explain them, put them in that context, and to tell us how the past has emerged, how changes have occurred. We are asking them to become historians, and what we're really tapping into is historical consciousness. So the question then becomes what is historical consciousness? Of course, there is a lot of literature on that, and I continue to go through that literature in many, many ways. But when I was in graduate school I worked with a man by the name of Warren Sussman. Warren was very interested in the interplay between ideology and myth, so I began to use Warren's ideas about ideology and myth within a structuralist context, the interest in ideology from Althusser, the interest in myth from Lévi-Strauss and knitting them all together in some kind of pattern. You know when you're very young you think this way. I would no longer think that way, but when you're young, you want to put the world together in a big way. You probably want to do it today. You're probably going to use this interview for some grand scheme of things, that's what the young do, that's what they should do. And so I had this in my mind, and so my first work essentially, I suppose, the work people still go to was a discussion of oral history in terms of the ways in which people made history under questioning and the interplay between ideology and myth. This kind of analysis meant a different role for the interviewer; the interviewer was deeply involved in the process. And a good deal of the literature at that time, especially in social sciences and oral history accented the abstracted, contemplative interviewer, that you were not to bias materials, you were to ask questions that were neutral, you were a cipher in the process, that everything depended upon the person being interviewed, and the questions if properly framed would not influence the testimony. Well, that was a lot of bullshit. Quite clearly what the interviewer does in an interview is crucial, and it's not only the fact that the person being interviewed articulates an ideology; the interviewer articulates an ideology in terms of the questions. If you examine the questions very carefully and look at them in context you can see what the ideology of the questioner is. Not an original thought on my part. Robert Merton and other people in sociology have been talking about this for years but the dominant trend in American sociology at the time was a kind of naive positivistic empiricism and that's essentially what I was arguing against. That had a certain kind of political dimension because of course out of the 1960s we had been arguing that theoretically as well, that kind of Marxist view of the world was anti-empiricist, so that all of these things kind of conspired at that moment in time in my life, that's between 1972 and 1979, and for me at the time in the United States that was kind of a lonely enterprise. I certainly had the support of Charlie Morrison who was my boss at the time who was very interested and encouraged me to go out and read and do this, that and the other thing, and of course cutting me the time to do this on the Ford Foundation project. But within the Oral History Association at the time, again I don't want to say dominant but certainly the most popular way of looking at the world was that kind of social-scientific view. If you were interested in memory, you were interested in memory as accuracy, if you were interested in the ideology it was to be found in the testimony, in the facts themselves. The truth of a statement was in the data itself and the interview was for information, and very few people concerned with things called texts or discourses. That language wasn't even around. So it was kind of a lonely enterprise. Then in 1979 there was the first international meeting on oral history held in Essex. For me, that was quite a revelation because I met a group of people, and I think it was for them too, we met each other: Luisa Passerini, Paul Thompson, mostly from the north Atlantic world, although one was from Mexico, but by and large from the north Atlantic world, and we found each other and we were working individually along a similar kind of trajectory that came out of the politics of the 1960s, a dissatisfaction with the dominant modes of thinking in the social sciences and opening to questions of narrative and text. Luisa by that time was working on her book on fascism, and if you look at that it opens up a discussion of the usefulness of Mikhail M. Bahtin, and the dialogic imagination and the nature of story. Luisa is very interested in that. Berteau had been working as a sociologist in qualitative sociology and very much in opposition to quantitative sociology as it was then called. So we had a kind of mutuality of experience, politically and intellectually, and we kind of found each other at Essex and that became a very important community, that community of oral history makers. It was oral history that essentially united us, and the field work experience, the joys of that field work experience, but the complications of that field work experience. We were all concerned that that field work experience be explored in all of its contingencies and contradictions and complexities. You know, it was not a simple relationship. It was a negotiating relationship; the negotiations were very, very complex and very complicated. I think we produced a body of work that still stands as a measure of at least a direction for oral historians to go. You said something about having read some of that work, and I think that's kind of interesting that someone at this stage in the 21$^{st}$ century would go back to work that was produced in the 1970s and 1980s as a kind of foundational work in oral history. I think that's because the questions we raised really are the questions to be asked in the practice.

**M. V.: You said a lot about my next question concerning the power of oral history. What do you feel about the power of oral history in this world?**

R. G.: We are at the meeting of the Oral History Association in which the theme is the revolutionary ideal. All kinds of people are talking about empowerment and I find it cute. In the older days I would argue for a much more careful and precise definition of what is meant by power. I do not believe people's lives are changed by being interviewed. On rare occasions, you know. In the 1970s we used to think that if we went out into the field we were also engaging in consciousness-raising. We were interviewing people and bringing them to historical consciousness. And that has some very serious consequences. One was what I would call false proletarianization. We believed that by raising the consciousness we were acting as the mentors of the working class and therefore we were members of the working class.

**M. V.: It's what I do now.**

R. G.: You know that whole language; you were probably raised on that language. I mean, looking back now it's Looney Tunes, we don't actually believe that kind of stuff. So I've always been a little careful about that. I'm not so sure if people's lives are changed by being interviewed. We interview people and certainly we ask them questions that they may not have ever thought were questions. We certainly turn the daily into something that is an object of investigation. We ask people to tell us things that they never thought were really questions. So there's not doubt that that happens, but then leave the interview, they go back to their family lives, they go back to working in that factory, they go back to sexist relationships, they go back to the world in which they live. So I don't know about what this empowerment in the interview might mean. Certainly in some cases it certainly leads people to question what has been unquestioned in their lives. In that sense, there is certainly intellectual powerfulness about that. Such a consideration is one, of many, ways in which oral history fieldwork merges in incredibly complex ways subjectivity and objectivity. While a full discussion of these issues is impossible here (I am now in the middle of reading, after many years of hesitation, Luce Irigaray The Sharing of Speech, which I might recommend to anyone who wants to pursue the sharing of authority) on the many complicated issues swimming around issues of the subject and the object in our speaking to one another.

For now, I would simply like to point out a deeper problematic in our work than populist ideas of power, important as they might be.[70] In some cases, and there's plenty of evidence here, people talk about community oral history projects where people get involved in doing their own history, where members of the community are actually, I don't want to say trained, but encouraged to become oral historians,

---

70) The whole question of subjectivity assumes greater importance when one realizes that many of the changes in thinking about oral history that I mentioned in the 2007 interview are really issues of the special role that oral history can play in uncovering subjective meanings of self, identity etc., issues that Passerini raise in her early work and issues that have continued to be the focus on much of our thinking as exemplified in Lynn Abrams latest work on oral history theory. (Comment by Ronald Grele on the occasion of English reprint of the book, October 16, 2012.)

RONALD GRELE

to go out and do their own history, and people taking control of their own history. That's somewhat different than an academic coming into a community, doing a history of the community and going away and writing a book. Now you have people in the community who are doing their own history, and our job is to encourage them and help them to do it the way it's going to be a better history, meaning it's going to explain more. That is another sense of empowerment, where the power of interpretation moves from the academy to the community, but it's a power of interpretation. It does not necessarily mean there's going to be a shift in the economic social or political forces at play in that community. It may happen, it may not. It may happen that on a community history project people sit around and they suddenly realize that they have a certain kind of political position vis-à-vis the forces of power in that community. It is a moment in what we used to say, the struggle for position. It could be a moment of that. So I think the whole discussion of power has to be talked about in a much more precise and careful manner than it is here. I attended a session where young people, I thought they were 14 or 15, turns out to be their college professors, were talking about interviewing their own parents who are migrant farm workers. And certainly, what they talk about is an experience that they had talking to their own families about the past of the family and certainly the joys that they found in that and the excitement were real. One young woman was in tears, she was so happy when she had interviewed her grandfather. That's real, but is it power? To translate that into questions of power, I don't know. I think one has to be much more careful about what the steps are.

**M. V.: My next question is related to this. Sometimes, those who are doing oral history in the Czech Republic hear some skeptical voices about methods, especially from the conservative historians, that oral history is too subjective, that memory is selective. How would you answer these voices?**

R. G.: My answer to that is we're asking important questions. The problem is they're asking unimportant questions. They have elaborated schemes for asking uninteresting questions. We unfortunately are working off the seat of our pants to ask all the important questions. The important questions are questions of subjectivity, questions of consciousness, questions of ideology, questions of identity. Those are the important questions. The important questions are not questions of fact; the important questions are not questions of data. The important question is how people live in history, how people create their pasts. I am fascinated by the ways in which people create stories. We've all moved to discussions of narrative these days. If I had to do the work that I used to do now, I would not be talking about language; I'd be talking about narrative. It's a different kind of thing. We're fascinated by how people formulate stories, and how people are creatures of story. My friend Jerry Brunner says that's what makes us human. Those, I think, are the important questions. I've never felt that oral historians should apologize for what they do, and again in the early days that put me at odds within the Oral History Association and other places because a great deal of the literature was apologetic. How we can be more precise like the social sciences, how can we convince people that really people do remember things? I've never felt that we should apologize for that. If you read Portelli the fascinating part of memory is that people don't remember things correctly, you know. Why don't they? What's going on? What is happening? In the same way that I tried to figure out what was going on in the Ford Foundation interviews. What lies were people telling themselves? What world were they imagining? The world of the imagination? Those are the important questions, I think.

**M. V.: I heard your talk in Sydney in 2006 about the future of oral history. You talked about the globalization problem. My question is about the future of oral history and the oral historian. What do you think about this?**
R. G.: Well, I have a kind of jaundiced view. It's quite apparent here that people see the future of oral history in terms of digitization and new technology. In fact, next year the media's going to be all about, the new technology. And a good deal of discussions that have gone on here, theoretical discussions, have been discussions about how

RONALD GRELE

to deal with the new technology, what the meaning of the new technology is. Even on the ethics panel yesterday there were questions about the ethics of the new technology. One of the things about the old Oral History Association was that it had a fetish with how to process things. What kind of paper to use how to build a transcript, proper methods of archiving and indexing, etc. But the issues were historiographical. The issues are history. We may be moving into a new technological age but the question is still a historical question. We should be concerning ourselves more with the historiographical and the historical questions revolving around what we call globalization. People talk here about marginalized people, etc. Margins are open to many kinds of definitions. The way they're using it here, they're talking about people who have been marginalized from our main stream, and they're talking about migrants, and the gay world, and they're talking about transgender people, and they're talking about African Americans and they're talking about racial minorities. But if we look at it as people who live on a margin of something or rather, where they meet other people who are living on the margins and we think about the global world as a world of marginality. People move all over the place, people have many kinds of identities. We live in a world in which there's an enormous movement in space and in time, and so that we all in a sense meet each other on the margins of something. And we have to explore how those margins have been created, how we live on those margins, how we explain ourselves to other people on that margin. Then we want to understand, say, in the United States, the ways in which young Hispanic people and young American people, young English speaking Americans are evolving a whole plateau that's half English, half Spanish. They're not maintaining the purity of the Spanish language in the United States. They are developing a language that's half-Spanish, half-English, etc. So they can talk to each other on the margins of things and the ways in which young Hispanic kids are adopting black attitudes. Something's happening in the mix places. You go to Dublin and you see all these Italians living in Dublin. What is happening in Dublin, to these Italians, to the Irish, what is going on there? Certainly, the Italians are marginal to Ireland but something is happening on the margins that are of historiographical interest. We can mobilize the new technology to better help, assist us in creating the kind of documentation of that marginality, if you will. But the real questions are historiographical questions. And my concern is that in the future, you're talking about this technological future, we lose sight of the fact that the questions are historiographical, the questions are historical questions.

**M. V.: I have one last question, which is more of a voluntary question: Do you have any recommendations or advice or message for Czech oral history or the Czech Oral History Association? If you have something on your mind that could be useful...**

R. G.: Well, I'll tell you certain kinds of concerns I have. I was in Jena being interviewed by a group of young people and I was quite shocked at the ways in which they turned their back on the whole body of theoretical literature. Post-communist Europe has become post-Marxist Europe and those people had never read Marx. To me, that's missing out on something that was very exciting. It may be that I'm just old fashion, that that period is gone and there's no more usefulness in it. I was quite surprised at what they weren't reading out of what I took to be a great tradition. And it doesn't necessarily have to be Marx. I have gone back to rereading it, and again, I'm interested in myth and I think I've explored the etymological side of myth enough and I'm kind of worried about that. So I'm going back and reading on myth to look for something different... But what struck me was that it was a name unknown, and maybe I'm old, I'm trapped in dead literature, dead traditions or something. But I was concerned about that, that people weren't mining a certain tradition for new insights. I still think there are wonderful insights to gain from continental literature. I'm also concerned with some of my colleagues who are so interested in sub-altern histories, etc. where certain kinds of connections are made with other bodies of data... Well, what do I want to say? They should read the literature of their time and they should read the literature of the past time.

**M. V.:** According to you, to what extent is it possible/recommendable to share a narrator's story, as it is discussed for example in Michael Frisch's "Shared Authority"?[71]

**R. G.:** Sharing a narrator's story, shared authority. As I noted above, the idea originated in a concept of shared authorship. The words might have been new at the time they were articulated but the idea was not necessarily so. The idea that an oral history was a joint creation of the interests of a historian realized in the questions asked and the various responses to the answers to those questions and the vision or memory of the interviewee formulated as a story or a series of responses that when woven together became a narrative. But, over time, shared authority came to stand for many other forms of interaction in the interview. As you know there has been a large and continuously growing literature exploring every aspect of what is meant by shared authority. I think it is important that we keep in mind the term "shared" because to my eye much of the literature concentrates on the authority of the narrator and his or her interpretative authority and rights in the creation while obscuring a discussion of the authority of the historian. A major exception this is, of course, Portelli who over and over reminds us that we and the people we talk with are parties to the tender negotiations that are involved in the oral history interview. Here, negotiation is the key for it is not clear that a shared authority results in some kind of agreement or consensus. What is at heart of the process is the recognition of difference – our recognition that the people we talk to have their own ways of interpreting their pasts and have the right to do so in whatever manner they are accustomed to do or the right to know what they know. But, equally, they just understand that we are struggling to know the world and we are not obliged to view the world as they would, that we have a different kind of knowledge of the past.

All of this does bring into question the way in which we have traditionally viewed our knowledge of the past. It is the glory of

---

71) A new question for the English edition of the book. Ronald Grele's answer delivered via email, October 17, 2012.

oral history that fundamentally tells us about our interaction with the world not the nature of the world itself. True, in many cases we can use the interview to amend and correct past interpretations of what happened at what time and in what place, especially in the case where we are talking with people who have never had a chance to leave a record for "history", but that is very narrow task and not the most interesting one. The most obvious example is the ways in which we talk of memory, not as accurate or inaccurate but as construction, as the active force of remembering. We understand interaction from our own lives and the research we do as a part of our lives as historians, the people we talk with understand interaction through having lived through events and spaces that we do not know and can only understand through them. The oral history interview is a unique meeting place of those understandings. It is not only possible for us to try to understand the narrator's story as you put it, it is fundamental that we do so. We will, of course, never fully understand that story as they understand it having lived it but it now strikes me as I write this out that they might understand our understanding as they examine the products we produce: books, articles, films, videos etc. Many, many complications that, I hope, can lead to other discussions.

**M. V.: How does oral history co-exist in the environment of journalists who refer to themselves as documentary-makers (if their work may be considered oral history) and the academic environment? I am asking this because some Czech so-called documentary-makers don't care much about historical accuracy or ethics towards the narrators. Has it been or is it still like this in your country?[72]**
R. G.: Firstly, let us be clear what we mean by historian. Doing history is not limited to those with advanced degrees affiliated with universities. History is one of the most democratic of disciplines. Almost everyone can become a historian. So, let us admit that when we talk about journalistic documentarians we are talking about people who

---

72) A new question for the English edition of the book. Ronald Grele's answer delivered via email, October 17, 2012.

RONALD GRELE

seek to come to some understanding of the past and present that understanding to a broad public. So, I think my easy answer to your question is that we should treat that product as we would treat any attempt to interpret the past, bringing to bear what we know as historians, what the discourse has been and is currently.

We all know of many historians who don't rack their brains over accuracy and ethics. Why should we expect anything different from documentarians? But I think your question actually centers on what one thinks are the differences between history and journalism. Too great an issue to be explored here. As I look at what passes for oral history in the United States and in many other countries, my discomfort is directed more at publications and other presentations that assume that the interviews speak for themselves. The most obvious example here is StoryCorps where thousands of people have been interviewed, portions of those recordings are played on radio and several books of just interviews have been published. To my mind these works represent an abnegation of responsibility on the part of the "historian" authors who have an obligation to tell us how such testimony helps us in understanding our past. I know this does not address itself to issues of accuracy and ethics. As far as accuracy is concerned that is why we have peer review and critics. Here, most sponsors of oral history fieldwork projects are governed by review boards that can impose sanctions and have rules and regulations on the interactions between interviewers and narrators. Oral history is exempt formally but most places impose these rules on fieldworkers. In addition the Oral History Association has a set of goals and guidelines that try to cover some ethical questions. It is still a sticky area. But I have some concerns that the discussion of ethics is, in many cases, a way of avoiding difficult methodological questions.

## DANIELA KOLEVA

"Whose voice do we hear when we give voice?"

Daniela Koleva is Associate Professor at the Department for History and Theory of Culture, the University of Sofia. Her research interests are in the field of oral history and anthropology of socialism and post-socialism, biographical and cultural memory, biographical methods, social constructivism. She published a monograph on the "normal life course" in communist Bulgaria *Biography and Normality* (Bulgarian, 2002) and a number of book chapters and articles in peer-reviewed international journals. Recent (co)edited volumes include *Negotiating Normality: Everyday Lives in Socialist Institutions* (Transaction, 2012) and *20 Years after the Collapse of Communism: Expectations, Achievements and Disillusions of 1989* (Peter Lang, 2011, ed. with N. Hayoz and L. Jesien). Her current work is on vernacular memory of socialism in Bulgaria, and religious and secular life-course rituals in the United Kingdom, Romania and Bulgaria.

### Interview with Daniela Koleva[73]

**M. V.: Do you remember the moment when you met oral history, the method, or when you used it for the first time?**

D. K.: I do, I remember exactly the moment, only at that moment I didn't know this thing was called oral history. It was, I think, in 1994, mid 1990s. We were sitting with my colleagues one afternoon over coffee and talking about life (about everyday life and life as such, not about academic life). And we realized that life was changing radically before our eyes: things that we had considered given, immutable, never changing before had begun to radically change, dramatically change after the 1989 revolution. So, for instance, we talked that we almost had forgotten about queues, that we were used to standing in huge queues only a couple of years before that. We had begun to

---

73) Interview with Daniela Koleva (D. K.) was recorded by Miroslav Vaněk (M. V.) in Lisbon, Portugal, February, 2008.

DANIELA KOLEVA

forget about shortages. We had begun to forget what ingenuity was required of us as mothers and wives to put together a meal out of products that were not available in the shops. We remembered that as students, we had to take a special course each year to enhance our "political maturity", that is, the knowledge of the ideological postulates of Marxism-Leninism and the history of the communist party. Our students had not even heard of those. So that was how the idea came to talk to people, mostly elderly people, who remembered that time, who remembered what it was like to live back then in that past. And the idea was more like what we call salvage anthropology or rescue archaeology – the efforts to find and preserve cultural information before a site was obliterated by new construction and the traces of that culture were lost forever. We felt that there was a distinct culture, a whole way of life, that was disappearing already at that moment and we wanted to capture what was left of it and we wanted to capture it in the memories of our interviewees and preserve it for future generations just to know.

So the first impetus was not a research one, we didn't have a specific research project or research question in mind. The first impetus was rather an archival one. We just wanted to document and to preserve these stories because we were able to see how big the changes were and how fast they were occurring and we understood that in just a couple of years nothing of the past reality as we remembered it, as we had it till 1989, would be left. So that was when I first met with oral history and it began with great enthusiasm and with a small project funded by the Bulgarian Ministry of Education and Science in 1995, which was called Experienced History. So we were interested in recent history, and more specifically in the history of everyday life as people experienced it and as people remembered it. Only later when we started interviewing and when we started to try to make sense of what we had, of the material that we had, only later I came to, I came across Paul Thompson's *The Voice of the Past* and somewhat later *The Oral History Reader* and some other publications. And only then I realized that what we had been doing was called oral history, and that there was this tradition and there were very interesting and fascinating studies that had been done and a vibrant international community of oral historians, these very nice people whom I came to know personally already. So that's how it began.

**M. V.: If you see some power which is home to the oral history discipline, what do you think is the most important? Why do we, or you or me, use oral history? What do you see is the most important, from this view, with regard to power?**

D. K.: Yes, of course I do. Of course. I think oral history is a powerful research method. I shall say a fruitful genre of research; otherwise I wouldn't have done it more than ten years already. Well, the first thing, as I mentioned, it can give us knowledge that we cannot find in the archives. This has been the first advantage of oral history that I have discovered and the first impetus to start doing oral history. This is knowledge about the everyday lives, about the underprivileged groups, like minority groups, ethnic and religious minorities, like marginalized groups, for instance disabled people. Like women – as you know, feminist history relies very much on oral history. And, very importantly in a post-communist context, knowledge of realities and experiences that were at odds with the established communist model and were suppressed before. So first of all, it gives us knowledge that is inaccessible in any other ways. Second, it gives us the possibility to have a more democratic research agenda. When we interview people, when we talk to people, we leave an open possibility for them to set their own agendas, to talk about things that they are interested in, to talk about what is important to them and not only what is important to us. So we can get these correctives from our "subjects of research" which I think is very democratic and it is really an ethos of doing historical and social scientific research that I fully embrace. So that's also very important to me. And also it has been personally enriching, really enriching for me, to talk to people who are, in a way wise, having lived through such profound transitions during their lives: after the Second World War and after the end of the Cold War. And they have been mostly what we call "ordinary people" but they have their wisdom and they have their ethics and I feel, as a person, I have been enriched by talking to them and listening to their stories. These are my benefits as a person, in addition to my benefits as a scholar.

**M. V.: Sometimes, those who are doing oral history in the Czech Republic hear some skeptical voices about methods, especially from the conservative historians, that oral history is too subjective, that memory is selective. How would you answer these voices?**
D. K.: Yes, yes, I also have heard such skeptical voices. In fact, the first occasion that I remember oral history appeared, the expression "oral history" and the method of oral history, was presented in a Bulgarian historical journal, in a critical review article of an oral history project and the publication that resulted from it. And the critique, written by a well-established professor, was just this, that the testimonies given in people's life stories were partial and subjective and we cannot rely on them, we had better go to the archives and so on. But, as I said, we cannot find everything in the archives – that's for one. Then, Paul Thompson wrote in *The Voice of the Past* about the growing awareness that "the written document has lost its innocence" – if it ever had one. So we have to be critical to written documents and just in the same way we have to be critical, and we are critical to oral documents, the ones that we produce together with our interviewees. We have to critically analyze the situation in which they appeared, the social position of the people who are talking to us. And we know that this social position influences their stories and we know how this works. So we can have this all in mind and be critical to oral sources in the same way as we are critical to all other sources. And then, most importantly, using oral sources and relying on memory means also a different kind of research program. You may have noticed that the concept of "memory" has become very popular in the last ten to fifteen years. Many historians speak about memory which, I think, is a result of that postmodern or let's say poststructuralist critique of history, saying that history is not the narrative of the past, history is one of the narratives of the past, and not necessarily the most privileged one. And when we talk about memory, we have in mind this relativization of the truth, that is there is no truth with a capital T which is always valid and always the same and to which

we are bound to arrive only through rigorous research procedures. I like Luisa Passerini's observation about the kind of truths we deal with, and I often remind it to my students: that all autobiographical memory is true; our task is to find out for whom and in what sense. So this is a way to contextualize our findings. To admit that the truths we uncover depend on their context, depend on the standpoint of their authors. This is a more modest position as a researcher, rather than the omniscient researcher who is like a god, who is somewhere above everything, above history, above ordinary people, and who can, who is privileged to see everything as it was. Come on, we are just ordinary people. And we are just, or we can be as biased as everyone else. Our only privilege is that we are self-reflexive, and self-critical, and we know that we are biased. And we somehow can, if we want to, find some ways to admit this bias and see how it might affect our interpretations and the conclusions we draw.

**M. V.: How do you see the future of oral history? What do you think about future development? Do you see some dangerous moments?**
D. K.: As you have noticed already I am an enthusiast about oral history. And I hope that the future of oral history is bright. I know that there are problems that have already been discussed for the past few years: different problems related to methodology, research ethics, related to the issues of the so called "empowerment". We often say we are giving voice to disadvantaged people, to marginalized groups and so on. And there are problems with that, because one of the questions that we can ask is probably: whose voice do we hear when we give voice? Sometimes these marginalized groups have interiorized dominant discourses about themselves and it is not so simple to just give voice and hope that we are democratic and that we are necessarily behaving like good researchers and good citizens, let's say. Saying this, I am aware that there are also tensions between the claim of oral history to be a scholarly endeavor, a scholarly exercise, to reach some kind of scholarly results on the one hand, and the democratic ethos of oral history on the other. The claim that oral history gives voice, that it is a democratic endeavor as well as an academic enterprise. Here I can see conflicts between its academic stance, its scholarly

DANIELA KOLEVA

position on the one hand, and its, let's say, political in the broad sense, political position, on the other. And I know that there are, there can be many ways to solve this problem; and one way was the one that Marx did, claiming that the position of the proletariat was the privileged one and the proletariat had "ownership", as they say now, of the historical truth. But to be honest now, I do have doubts about it and it doesn't seem a universal solution.

**M. V.: I have one last question an almost voluntary one because it is a little bit connected with my personal experience. When we met in person the first time in Berlin, you influenced me very positively. I was so energized by it. So I would like to ask you if you can advise or say something to younger Czech oral historians or to the new Czech Oral History Association.**

D. K.: Well, of course. Giving academic advice is part of my job so I am always ready with some advice, I don't know who will follow it if anybody but, you know, I am thinking of a famous American cultural anthropologist from the first half and the middle of the twentieth century, Alfred Kroeber. In his heyday Alfred Kroeber was asked what he would advise anthropologists who were going to do field research. And he was not very polite he said, "What is there to advise? People either can do it, or they cannot do it." I think Kroeber was not right; people can learn to do it. There are very good guidebooks, guidelines, there is very good methodology and people can try and learn to do it very professionally. But even if they learn to do it, they won't be successful if they are not really willing to do it. So my advice is: make sure that you want to do oral history and then it will work.

**M. V.: In your view, to what extent is it possible/recommendable to share a narrator's story, as it is discussed for example in Michael Frisch's "Shared Authority"?[74]**

D. K.: I haven't found a universal answer to this question. Each time it seems to depend on the situation and on the kind of publication.

---

74) A new question for the English edition of the book. Daniela Koleva's answer delivered via email, October 19, 2012.

I have published 5–6 collections of life stories where I have written only a preface, sometimes a really small one, in other cases a very substantial interpretative piece. In most of these collections, the interviewees appear with their names, which have been their own wish, of course. In two collections, they are kept anonymous. This is already a different level of co-authorship perhaps. Our own interpretative works are still another case. I have always tried to acknowledge the participation of the interviewees and to "give them the floor". Usually this has been relatively unproblematic as I have mostly interviewed ordinary people, many of them repressed by the former regime. The situation was different in the last project (still on-going) where we focus on middle-level communist nomenclature. Here, the question of empathy is completely different.

**M.V.: How does oral history co-exist in the environment of journalists who refer to themselves as documentary-makers (if their work may be considered oral history) and the academic environment? I am asking this because some Czech so-called documentary-makers don't care much about historical accuracy or ethics towards the narrators. Has it been or is it still like this in your country?[75]**
D. K.: There have been quite a few documentaries in Bulgaria, all of them using interviews to a greater or lesser extent. Some are more matter-of-fact, others have more complex and subtle messages. Some have historians as consultants, others don't. I have no problems with that. Oral historians are not the gatekeepers to people's memory. The rest is a question of professionalism, professional ethics and good creative ideas. But of course, whenever this is not the case, you can criticize the documentary from a historical point of view. Journalists are not the gatekeepers of the public intellectual space either.

---

75) A new question for the English edition of the book. Daniela Koleva's answer delivered via email, October 19, 2012.

DANIELA KOLEVA

# ELIZABETH MILLWOOD

"We don't listen well in our societies."

 Elizabeth Millwood holds a B. A. and an M. A. from Oakland University. Since 1997, she has worked for the Southern Oral History Program (Center for the Study of the American South) in the University of North Carolina. A specialist in oral history methods, she has run training programs for aspiring oral historians around the state and the region, and has spoken on oral history techniques at numerous professional gatherings. She was the 2004 recipient of the Robert E. Bryan Public Service Award, given by the University of North Carolina for inspiring and practical work in the North Carolina community.[76]

## Interview with Elizabeth Millwood[77]

**M. V.: Do you remember the moment when you decided to begin doing oral history?**

E. M.: I'd be happy to start with that, I really don't see myself as a mother of oral history, but consider myself in the second generation. I was thinking through when I first encountered oral history. At some time in the 1980s, I read an article by a historian who'd done some writing in Michigan. They had interviewed automotive workers and they were using that in a larger setting to explain the transformation that happened in labor and the drama and the voices of the people coming from farms in the south of the United States and who had moved north to work on automotive lines. It was one of those sorts of snap moments where I said, "These people are just everyday people and yet their voices bring so much understanding to me about what their lives were about." And that initially started my interest. Then I began methodically finding out what is this oral history and met

---

76) Information based on: Southern Oral History Program [online] [2013-01-04]. <http://www.sohp.org/content/staff/>.
77) Interview with Elizabeth Millwood (E. M.) recorded by Miroslav Vaněk (M. V.), Prague, Czech Republic, February, 2007.

with the head of the Michigan Oral History Association, an elderly lady who just talked about how important this was and how critical it was and not many people were doing it. From there on, I moved into graduate work with Charlie Morrissey. It was a matter of years and making connections and deciding what this is about. And then when I moved to North Carolina, I got connected and started an oral history program.

**M. V.: Can you describe or summarize the program? What were its main aims?**

E. M.: It started in 1973 and its main heart has been Jacqueline Hall who is the director. Her approach to oral history is very much the bottom up approach, that of laborers, field workers, tobacco workers, those are the voices of oral history. And so her driving force from the beginning has been very much in synchrony to what oral history is about – these voices of the everyday people. And part of her impetus is beyond just publication, beyond making sure that the sound is recorded, but to link our work back to the people where we have used their voices. And so often our work is taken back in performances and plays and videos and things like that, returned to these communities, because so many of these communities are not well off in many ways.

**M. V.: What is the power of oral history?**

E. M.: I have often a sort of wondering about the power of it. It is hard to describe it without sounding both emotional and non-analytical. You go and see someone telling a story or hear someone telling a story and you are in their presence where often emotion infuses all of their words. If you've done your research and you can go in and probe and ask them to clarify things they will often tell you, "No, you are wrong, the way you are thinking about this is wrong." That inter-action is critical to our research and critical to our understanding. And this is a gift. I have often told community groups that we don't listen well in our societies. And if you go in and you are given this chance to ask questions and you can learn more about something, people are so thrilled because you are listening to them. Well, you need to correct facts, you do need to have solid grounding, but the power is that you're there able to make inquiry, you're there able to expand on something. It might be clear that there is some stepping back from the topic, but the power is really a human connection and listening and that's so important.

Part of the strength of oral history is that, in my thinking, it is more of a methodology that can bring to discussion a range of disciplines. And I would see that if it became bogged down in being a discipline, it might lose some of its energy and creativity and diversity in many ways. So, after some years of sitting on the fence, I decided that methodology is the appropriate way to look at it. One of the things that I see, and this may be leaping ahead in terms of thinking, it's one of the challenges of oral history, such an egalitarian approach when people access people. One of the challenges, especially in the future, is an art and craft and training in the methodology in the sense that not everyone who has a microphone should think or say that they are in oral history.

**M. V.: In the Czech Republic, we have been strongly criticized by conservative historians who say that oral history is very subjective, that the memory of narrators is selective. Is it the same in the United States?**

E. M.: It is a great question. I believe that oral history met with much of the same skepticism in the U.S., and I think that you can still find some fairly conservative academics who would say that it's too subjective to be used as primary testimony. But my reaction to that is very simply: it will never be the only source of historical memory; it should be matched with and challenged by paper documents and other resources. In that sense it is just an added color in the overall spectrum of history. Yes, there are a lot of arguments that can be made or that the telling of my story will be subjective. But if a researcher has had time to mine and dig down into the documentary record then he or she is able to say, for instance: "Well, the other view is this, what's your thought about that." And we don't have that opportunity with paper record. It's not a complete and total answer and it is subjective. But I also think that oral history has been very much helped by further research in memory studies and in looking at how we tell our story over periods of time, how we tell a certain story, how we refine it. And how, especially around traumatic issues, we find ways to sort, refine them and get them more comfortable to tell. All of that relates to how the human brain works and thinks. We have people we interviewed 30 years ago, and we go and interview them again, and it becomes a new set of perspectives.

**M. V.: What do you think about the future of oral history? I think that there are new challenges – globalization, digitalization.**
E. M.: From the perspective of someone who works a lot in the oral history community, where we train volunteers, where I bring them access to what the academy knows and how to think about oral history, transfer to digital has created some new variations. If preservation is one of our goals, which has to be one of our goals, the transformation to digital has made that more complex and more dangerous. I agree that we should stayed on the other side of the digital. I just see great flexibility of what this new technology brings us. But the concern is that in the oral history community they are often funded in a very small way, they are doing preservation at a local library. We have tried working with some of the groups to assist a project to the level that is something we want to deposit in our materials because we have broader options for access to large dark archives, digital storage and mass storage that many of these communities don't have; that's one aspect. So one big challenge is the issue of preservation. The other issue is, I don't know how to frame this, and it is something that I mentioned before. It's as documentary work and oral history has to try to persuade and encourage people to do their research and do their background material. Many fine undergraduate programs encourage students to do documentary works. What they are doing is essential but with no context, with no idea of how these changes are different. It would be great to broaden and deepen it. I think that as we continue to make oral history accessible, but with a secondary encouragement, it doesn't always have to be exquisitely detailed complex research, it can be done at specific community levels, where craft training and background is really important. I don't know if I'm

explaining that well but my concern is that if we are going to do this and expend this labor, it should be done well.

**M. V.: We don't want "only" to collect recorded and transcribed material; we would like to interpret it, too. Is it the same or similar in the United States? I think that there are three ways and objectives to use oral history research: collecting, digitalization and archiving. Then some researchers use this material for their own interpretation; and finally, edited interviews are published for general public.**

E. M.: I would say, it's pretty much the same here. What I see from the community side is a broader and increasingly common impulse to do oral history and then throw it up immediately on the web. Those projects often do not pay good attention to either writing about what they are doing or preserving what they are doing. They are just doing it and making it available. But there is one very good thing in the U.S.; the trend to make the material available and to analyze it at the same time is growing. So you have not only your transcript and your sound up; you can also go in and as a researcher from the Czech Republic you want to read an interview that we've done. So, you can go in and selectively begin to say, "I want this and this and that." And you can go to that part in the interview where your topic is discussed. Those are expensive but helpful tools.

The other extreme is that simple, "we are doing the oral history here". It is here, listen. For people to encounter the power of oral history, it is still a very minimal use. But using it in a performance, as just bringing the voices back to people in performances, it helps them to understand what it was like for the workers. But it is one of my curiosities, and I know you and I have discussed this before, to know how much more work in the Czech Republic you have to do to get people to trust you and open up to you, in terms of you're not a family member or good friend of them, just someone who is recording.

**M. V.: You say that one way of publication is that you can take an interview and put it on the web. Do you have any difficulties be-**

cause there is confidential information in the interview? We have a law in the Czech Republic that stops private information from being open to the public. Maybe, because you are without this problematic past, the U.S. is more open than the Czechs. Do you think you have these problems? As for me, I have great concerns about publishing unauthorized interviews; it's contradictory to research ethics.

E. M.: I absolutely agree with some of your concerns. I think putting unfiltered interviews up on the web is one of the better uses. In part, it becomes a great deal of information that you just have to wade through yourself, you have to listen to all two hours of interview yourself. The other downside is that, and I criticize gently, that many of these projects which post interviews in this way do that just to make material accessible, just because they don't have resources but they have web access and web technology skills. Then very small community projects, with six voices for example, can talk about community history. But the downside is that an individual can completely give a release and refer to some character in a town setting in not a nice way. How many meanings can be taken from a criticism of the local mayor? I wouldn't see that level of sophistication.

**M. V.: Do you have any recommendations for Czech oral historians? What message would you give them? What is important?**

E. M.: What I see as your advantage is a huge fertile ground that you have around here, with all these memories that have not been recorded. Gathering them into one piece of work has a potentially wonderful value. Help your society, people; teach people to understand in every way, daily, weekly, monthly how important their history is. I think some of the best ways to do this is to point at the importance of their own story. Sometimes you have to persuade them about the importance of their own story, it's incredibly powerful. In any culture, there is a certain percentage of people not interested in history and the other that thinks it is stupid, and then another who thinks it is all made up and therefore there is no need to know anything about it. But when individuals understand that they are historical actors or their parents were, the power of that understanding is evident. As a friend of mine was saying yesterday: he lived in this culture, he was born in 1962, within the home he could discuss things, but at school he couldn't discuss things. To reunite, to knit together this history again, I think that's where the organization you formed was about, and what Czech historians can really bring back to their own people.

**M. V.: To what extent, in your view, is it possible to share a narrator's story, as it is discussed for example in Michael Frisch's "Shared Authority"?[78]**

E. M.: "Shared authority" is a rich topic that defies simple descriptions or prescriptions. I strongly recommend the special section on Shared Authority in the Winter/Spring 2003 Oral History Review. Now ten years old, the diverse essays and comments highlight the philosophical, ethical and structural challenges in sharing authority.

**M. V.: How does oral history co-exist in the environment of journalists who refer to themselves as documentary-makers (if their work may be considered oral history) and the academic environment? I am asking this because some Czech so-called documentary-makers do not concern themselves with historical accuracy or ethics. Has this been or is it similar in your country?[79]**

E. M.: As I note in my 2007 interview, the lines between oral history and documentary work are often imprecise in public understanding. With the constantly expanding interest in documentary work, I encourage anyone who asks to bring oral history research methods to a documentary project. In many cases, documentarians may be working with an individual who will only be interviewed once which heightens the importance of creating an appropriately researched and grounded interview.

---

78) A new question for the English edition of the book. Elizabeth Millwood's answer delivered via email, January 3, 2013.
79) A new question for the English edition of the book. Elizabeth Millwood's answer delivered via email, January 3, 2013.

# CHARLES T. MORRISSEY

"Basically I'm a doorkeeper; I open doors and let people into history. And that's very valuable for the future."

 Charles T. Morrissey, a Past President of the Oral History Association, began his career in 1962 by interviewing former members of the White House staff during the Truman administration for the Truman Library, and he subsequently directed the John F. Kennedy Library Oral History Project. He has also directed projects for and about the Ford Foundation, the Pew Charitable Trusts, the Howard Hughes Medical Institute, the Bush Foundation of Minnesota.[80] He is still, at age 79, a practicing oral historian at Baylor College of Medicine in Houston, Texas.

## Interview with Charles T. Morrissey[81]

**M. V.: Mr. Morrissey, I am so glad that we could meet here in Oakland – it is fascinating to me. And I would like to ask some simple questions, the first one is about oral history. Do you remember the moment when you encountered oral history, when you saw that it is a way for you?**

C. M.: I can't say that there was a precise moment at which that happened. I was a graduate student for four years nearby where we're meeting right now. I was at Berkley, the University of California at Berkley, and, of course, all graduate students in history and related disciplines are taught that you can trust the written word but you cannot trust the spoken word. And I found myself more and more skeptical of the written word in its authenticity, its credibility, in print. And if I went and interviewed somebody, I found there was a story that explained the creation of the document, why it has

---

80) Information based on: History Forum Lecture by Oral Historian Charles T. Morrissey [online] [2012-12-23]. <http://uah-history-events.blogspot.cz/2008/10/history-forum-lecture-by-oral-historian.html>.

81) Interview with Charles T. Morrissey (C. M.) recorded by Miroslav Vaněk (M. V.), Oakland, USA, October, 2007.

survived, what significance people have attached to it. And in many cases, the story revised the historian's sense of what is the significance of this, why does this document exist.

So I remember doing an interview within a two-minute walk of where we're meeting right now with a former member of the U.S. Senate, named William Noland, from California, and his family owned the newspaper, the Oakland Tribune, which was right across the street here. And he had left the Senate in 1958 to run for governor of California, and the governor of California had left the governorship to go to Washington as U.S. Senator. And both of them lost overwhelmingly in that 1958 election. Now the media was reporting that Senator Noland wanted to be governor so he could control the Republican delegation to the 1960 Republican Convention, and get the presidential nomination away from Richard Nixon. I interviewed him, and he denied this vigorously. But later, both his children said, "Father was obsessed with his presidential ambitions." So I thought, here's an interesting case where, basically, the press was reporting one thing, he was denying it, but other members of his family were affirming it. All of which simply emphasizes how complex historical research is, always much more complex than we anticipate at the outset. And by interviewing several people I was able to deny Noland's denial, and also deny the paper trail he had created that he really wanted to come back to California because he wanted to be "closer to his family", the excuse often offered.

So out of that came, to me, the very important point, you're always working with a mix of sources, a paper trail, a spoken memory trail, and you've got to get more than one interviewee on record in order to solve the complexity of it. That happened in 1960, that interview, and two years later I was hired and doing oral history interviews for the Harry S. Truman presidential library on people who had worked on the White House staff when Truman was president. Absolutely fascinating interviews on how the Truman administration made so many crucial decisions. And then I was doing that when John F. Kennedy was assassinated in November of 1963, and it's hard to believe, but in those days there were only two oral historians in Washington, DC doing oral history, and the other one was Forrest Pogue, who was committed to doing his multi-volume biography of General George Marshall. So, by default, I became director of the John F. Kennedy Library Oral History Project, and a career was born. It took a while for my head to catch up with the reality that a career was born, but here I am in 2007 still active in the oral history movement.

**M. V.: Congratulations. You did a lot of work, I see. The other question is about the power of oral history. Where is the power, what is the power of oral history?**

C. M.: Yes. Always think in multiples, I tell my students. There are several powers, one of which is obvious: it lets neglected people, neglected by historians, by historical documentation, get into history. So if history is the story of rich and powerful men, it allows poor women to get into the historical record. Secondly, I am convinced that the paper trail is largely a contrivance to cover actuality, not necessarily reveal it. Therefore, when you go into the interview, you can get someone to evoke the context in which the document was created. So you're constantly playing off the old-fashioned documentary resource that Leopold von Rocka told us was the source of all history. With the spoken recollection, which has its frailties – memory plays tricks on all of us – on the other hand, some people can come in and zero in precisely on why something happened the way it did that's quite contrary than the impression you would get from the paper trail. Those are the two primary ones. I'll mention third as a self-satisfaction, really, and that is: every oral historian, by asking questions, is co-creating a record, and that record wouldn't exist if you didn't exert the initiative to make it happen. So you're causing something to exist for the future that would not exist if you didn't help make it exist. And I find that very satisfying as the years go by. Basically I'm a door keeper; I open doors and let people into history. And that's very valuable for the future. I'm a historian with a strong sense of the future needs of historical knowledge.

**M. V.: I think that it's the normal way. We are somewhere at the beginning, maybe, compared to the U.S. and Great Britain. Sometimes we are attacked by conservative historians. They tell us, "Yes,**

CHARLES T. MORRISSEY

but there is too much subjectivity, there is a problem with the selectivity of the memory of the narrators." What is your response to this?

C. M.: Undeniably, memory is selective. Undeniably, those papers that get chosen to be saved are based on a very subjective decision. This is trash, we can throw it away; this is valuable, we should preserve it. Who makes those decisions on what basis? It's often a secretary who needs a clean file drawer, so she says, "I'll just junk all this paper. Who cares about this?" Well, historians care about this. So selectivity is a problem. On the other hand, I have found, in my interviewing technique, if I can say to people, you and I, working together, for the future, need to collaborate closely and make sure that I get your full story, all the details, example, illustrations as possible, because both of us are committed to serving the future as best as we can. And if people will buy into that collaborative relationship and not think of ourselves as rivals – my questions are perhaps too intrusive, or something like that – then, I think, by working jointly with good rapport between us, we can achieve something that is of value. Furthermore, to go back to my earlier point, never be satisfied with one interview with one person to totally document a situation. Multiple interviews with several people from different angles of vision will probably give you enough from which you can draw a consensus, and which a historian takes a deep breath and says, "Well, it must have happened this way."

**M. V.: Okay. My question is about the future of oral history. What do you think about the future of oral history, of oral historians? Is there some new challenge?**

C. M.: People, of course, are very divided on that question, and there are some who take the extreme position that we are going to find less, and less is put in a paper document or any other type of document, be it electronic or whatever, that's going to be preserved, and the only way you're going to get history back, 20, 30 years forward from today, is through the oral history interview process. Now, that's because there is so much concern, particularly in the United States right now, the fall of the year 2007, with the incredible resurgence of secrecy in federal government. A lot of lawyers in the USA are saying to their clients, "Put nothing in writing and throw away what you got." So, what does that leave the future historian, but letters that might read, "As we discussed on the telephone, please pursue the strategy we agreed on." What does that really tell you? Well, it doesn't tell you much unless you go to the people who had the telephone conversation, and "What was it that you agreed to?"

So, in that sense, I think the future for oral history is very bright. The new, probably primary, way of documenting the past and trying to analyze it and explain it. On the other hand, the public funding in this country for what I would call "humanistic activities", like historical research and explanation, is constantly decreasing. So you have to wonder, the basic financial question, where is the money going to come from to afford all this? And I think that's one of the big differences I've seen in my career, which is now forty-some years, the rise of the presidential library's many foundations, philanthropic foundations, being interested in preserving history as a cultural activity. I don't see as much of that now, and I'll probably see less of that in the immediate future, and that's very regrettable.

**M. V.: Yes. The last question is almost a voluntary question. Do you have any recommendations or advice for Czech oral history or the Czech Oral History Association…**

C. M.: I would take two that come to mind right off the top of my head. And one is, look for those gaps in your national history for which there is little, if any, documentation, and say, "I will find people who lived that experience and interview them to fill that gap." And the second one, if you're teaching students of all ages, enjoy the pleasure. Enjoy the pleasure of not just meeting people, talking with them, making a record of their lives, that has usefulness, not only for their own families, but for their communities, their country, whatever. And also bear in mind that human nature is such, every interview is unique. Every person is unique. So I've done hundreds of these, but I have to remind myself, on the edge of one that's forthcoming: this one is probably going to be different from all the others. And you've got to be prepared to go with the personality of the person you're dealing with. But out of these interviews, when they go well, I come with a great sense of exhilaration, great satisfaction that I was able to do this. And I urge your students to share the sense of satisfaction.

**M. V.: I would like to ask you two additional questions: 1) According to you, to what extent is it possible/recommendable to share a narrator's story, as it is discussed for example in Michael Frisch's "Shared Authority"? 2) How does oral history co-exist in the environment of journalists who refer to themselves as documentary-makers (if their work may be considered oral history) and the academic environment? I am asking this because some Czech so-called documentary-makers don't care much about historical accuracy or ethics towards the narrators. Has it been or is it still like this in your country?[82]**

C. M.: When contrasting journalistic interviewing and oral history interviewing I emphasize "archival" as the key word for distinguishing one question-asking type of inquiry from the other. For decades, when teaching oral history workshops in the USA, I have given students a ten-word definition of oral history: "Recorded interviews which preserve historically significant memories in archival form." Sometimes the final three words in this definition get revised so the then-word definition thus reads: "Recorded interviews which preserve significant memories for future use." This alternative language is more colloquial and avoids time-consuming digressions to archival concepts and practices when workshop attention should steadfastly focus on oral history skills and programs designs. But the pivotal point is still firmly anchored: memory-saving endeavors entail archival processing and custody to assure spoken reminiscence are not ephemeral. To borrow from Michael Frisch, oral history is truly a "shared authority" which produces co-created archival documents.

Yes, I readily describe my vocation as doing "archival" oral history, but ironically I have been writing for the past sixteen years a monthly

---

82) Questions for English reprint of the book. Charles T. Morrissey's answers delivered via letter from December 3, 2012.

column for the Hardwick Gazette, a weekly newspaper in Northern Vermont, 35 miles below the Canadian frontier. However, my role as a journalist functions separately from my enterprises as an oral historian. Admittedly there are similarities: oral history students have heard me say journalists and oral historian both ask six basic questions in all interviews: who did what, when and where, how and why. But still I maintain the memory-saving objective is distinctive from journalist gleaming present-centered newsworthy reports for their editors, and subsequently for their consumers.

Other differences are undeniable: oral history has to be collegial to be successful, whereas journalistic interviewing can often be adversarial. Oral historians urge their respondents to review transcripts editorially to correct errors and clarify intended meanings. These co-created archival documents, when properly deposited, are governed by legal agreements mutually derived and formally executed. Academic proposals for launching oral history projects in the USA must usually be approved by mandated Institutional Review Boards for Human Subject Research. Journalists can be heartily thankful they don't need to satisfy these impediments, often devised by biomedical researchers, who operate outside an ethos emerging from the humanities and social sciences.

Deliberating these ranging perspectives in a welcomed professional examination of varying viewpoints is certainly invigorating for everybody involved, globally, in oral history and journalism.

CHARLES T. MORRISSEY

## ROBERT PERKS

"There is a difference between the memory and the telling, and that's the infinitely fascinating part of oral history because it has to do with reasons for sharing memories, it has to do with power relationships between the teller and the listener and it's infinitely variable in the way in which people tell their stories and that's very interesting and it's a multiple identity that people have when they tell it at different times."

Dr Robert Perks has been Lead Curator of Oral History at the British Library since 1988, and Director of National Life Stories since 1996. He heads a team of some twenty staff involved in oral history fieldwork in a variety of sectors: from arts and crafts to business and finance, from the utilities to science, from architecture to publishing. He is the Secretary of the Oral History Society, a Visiting Professor at the University of Huddersfield, and Series Editor of the Oxford University Press Oral History Series. He acts as an advisor to the Heritage Lottery Fund, the Centre for Life History Research at the University of Sussex, the Australian Generations National Oral History Project (Monash University Melbourne), and the Canadian Oral History Centre at the University of Winnipeg. He is a previous Council Member of the International Oral History Association. Between 2002 and 2007 he was a Board Member of the Museums, Libraries and Archives Council South East.

An editor of *Oral History: The Journal of the Oral History Society*, his publications include *The Oral History Reader* (Routledge, 1998, second edition 2006), *Oral History, Health and Welfare* (Routledge, 2000), *Ukraine's Forbidden History* (Dewi Lewis Publishing, 1998), and numerous audio publications including *Voices of the Holocaust: a Cross-Curricular Resource Pack* (British Library, 1993), now a web-based resource, and *The Writing Life: Authors Speak* (British Library, 2011).

He was awarded a Winston Churchill Fellowship in 1992 to research nationalism, memory and oral history in Eastern Europe, and acted as a special historical advisor for the Council of Europe in Romania. He was co-ordinator of the Millennium Oral History Project, a collaborative initiative between the British Library and BBC Regional Broadcasting, and the largest oral history project ever mounted in Britain. In 2007 he was awarded an honorary DLitt by the University of Huddersfield in recognition of his work in the field.

## Interview with Robert Perks[83]

**M. V.: I would like to know how you came across oral history for the first time. What was the key moment that influenced you?**

R. P.: I think there are probably two moments in terms of oral history that were significant. One of the important things about my family is that my great-grandfather worked for Thomas Edison who invented recorded sound. He was an engraver working in Birmingham in the Midlands and he fell on hard times, I think, and migrated to America, where he worked for Thomas Edison. And I've always thought there was a family link right through from the history of recorded sound to what I do. I've always been interested in tape recorders. Since I was a kid I've had tape recorders, bought tape recorders, used tape recorders and microphones and have always been aware of that and recording things around me. And then I guess, like a lot of historians of my generation, oral history was never terribly significant when we were growing up and it was still a quite new methodology even when I was at university. And it was really only when I started to do research for PhD that I came across oral history and I came across Paul Thompson's *The Voice of the Past* and began to think about collecting people's stories. I was researching late 19th century, early 20th century political change in Britain and it was whilst I was doing that that I realized that there was information you could get from people's memories that simply wasn't available in printed forms like newspaper accounts, and manuscripts and other documents and so on. As a part of this, I was working on a particular firm in Yorkshire which was quite famous as a profit-sharing firm and it had a long history, so I put an advert in the

---

83) Interview with Robert Perks (R. P.) recorded by Miroslav Vaněk (M. V.), Oakland, USA, October, 2007.

ROBERT PERKS

paper just to see if anyone was around who remembered working at that particular company, and two or three people came forward and those were my first interviews and they were disasters. I didn't know what I was doing, I knew a little about equipment, but I wasn't working within any particular methodology. But it gave me a sense that what is locked up in people's memories is very unique and very special, but also very problematic: that the people disagree, memories disagree, and the type of evidence you can get from oral history is going to be problematic and difficult because when juxtaposed with other sources it often disagrees. But in a sense that was really what got my interest as a historical source and that's really where it started with me, with both the family background in terms of the technology, what is represented of recording sound, and a historian – or becoming a historian – of how oral history can juxtapose with traditional forms of historical inquiry.

**M. V.: What do you think is the power of oral history? Which are the positives of this method?**

R. P.: I think there are a number of things that oral history can provide. The first obvious one is that it gives us information that we can't get from other historical sources: simple. Particularly about people who have been ignored by traditional historical sources, or who have been marginalized by the majority of society, who have experiences which are not generally recorded by traditional ways of gathering data and so on. So it gives us more history. But I also think oral history gives you a different type of history which is to do with the way people express themselves and the way people make sense of their experiences, and how that changes over time. So it gives you both oral history and also a different kind of history. A lot of the work I've been involved in over the years has been to do with using oral history to empower people to tell those particular stories, so archives are created which otherwise wouldn't exist about ethnicity and women's experiences. But also it puts the ways of telling that story into the hands of people who do it themselves so they're telling the story as they want to tell it. And that's really important I think because it challenges archives and librarians and historians to think about it in a slightly different way.

**M. V.:** You said it, we have this problem in the Czech Republic, but it is not our problem, it is a general problem that half of the historical community has refused oral history because of the problem of narrator's memory that is too subjective. You know what I mean. I think that you had the same problem in England, would you say that they started talking about this?

**R. P.:** Well, for a long time we were quite defensive as historians arguing for the importance of oral history, but frequently people were criticizing the fallibility and the unreliability of memory as a historical source. But I think that what's happened is that we've been able to argue more clearly since the 1980s and onward thanks to people like Sandro Portelli and others that began to look at subjectivity and look at the relationship between the past and the present. I think now most historians understand oral history as a relationship between the present and the past. And because of the way in which people tell their memories is different from the memories themselves, the process between the remembering and the telling is extremely interesting for historians since people vocalize their stories in a particular way to a particular audience on a particular occasion representing a particular identity. So every time you interview someone over time, the way in which they make sense of their memory, or rather tell their memory, is going to be different. In other words, there is a difference between the memory and the telling, and that's the infinitely fascinating part of oral history for historians because it's to do with audience, it's to do with narrative form, it's to do with reasons for sharing those memories at particular times, it has to do with audience, it has to do with power, it has to do with power relationships between the teller and the listener and it's infinitely variable in the way in which people tell their stories. And that's very interesting and it's a multiple identity that people have which they tell at different times, and I think, certainly in the context of societies, former communist societies, former apartheid societies, and so on, oral history is a very valuable tool to rescue experience but also to tell it in different ways at different times. It's extremely valuable for those reasons.

ROBERT PERKS

**M. V.: What do you think about the future of oral history? How do you think it will continue?**

R. P.: Well, I think there are different futures for oral history. Although oral history is now a national movement and an international movement, and there are countries constantly picking up oral history, I think it's developing at different speeds in different places for different reasons. Certainly, in Britain one of the changes is that it started as a radical socialist, feminist movement as part of the social history in the 1960s, but it's become a very wide church now of activity. Oral history is being used by lots of different people: by religious historians, by medical historians, by corporate historians so it's very very broad now politically and socially and is being used by many many disciplines so it's becoming a methodology that is used more widely than we ever anticipated, and that's happened in other places in the world, but not all places in the world. I think certainly still in those societies where there was a period of oppression or political or social oppression, oral history is a very very valuable tool indeed. You can see it in South Africa and the former Soviet Union, and other countries around the world, and equally in societies where indigenous peoples have been oppressed. In Australia, for instance, with the "stolen" Aborigine generation experience, oral history has become a very valuable tool. I think the question is in societies like British society where it's not so obvious that oral history is a tool for social change. The challenge for us in the future will be to see how oral history will remain a radical tool rather than being absorbed into mainstream history. In a sense, we've always wanted it to be mainstream history so it has been an achievement that we've got to that point. But there's also a sense that oral history has sort of lost its radical edge as a political movement and maybe we need to keep an eye on whether we can keep oral history in the forefront of radical change as a social movement. So I think that's the flux that we're in Britain. But everywhere you go around the world I think you'll have different moments of development and different moments of change and different ways in which oral history is being used by different people for different purposes. So it's quite difficult to say what the future of oral history is. Certainly, I think that the technology for gathering high quality recordings of people is certainly much easier than it has ever been and increasingly more material is going to be used in web context so it goes around the world very quickly and can be used in different ways. But as we've been hearing [at this conference] there are some concerns about mass access to material if that means it can be abused for other purposes. Obviously within certain unstable societies where maybe the data collected can then be misused by security forces or political forces of various kinds, as oral historians we need to think very carefully about the implications of mass access of the material we've been collecting. I think in stable democratic countries, it's not perhaps something we've given too much attention to. But perhaps we should be in terms of the wide scale of implications of putting something on the web.

**M. V.: Is there something that you would recommend to Czech oral historians? Some advice or some message for the Czech oral history; something useful for us?**
R. P.: I think it's fantastic that you've established an association in the Czech Republic. I think it's important that people who work alone a lot of the time have an opportunity to come together to discuss things that hold them together. I'm trying to think of any mistakes that we made in the [UK] Oral History Society. I think it's important to be inclusive. One of the strengths of the British oral history movement is that it represents lots of different people who are using oral history. So even though there are lots of academics involved, it's not a wholly academic movement. There are lots of community historians involved, family historians, journalists, broadcasters, people working with older people in a caring context. It's very broad the membership of the British Oral History Society and also the journal we produce is deliberately aimed to be very inclusive, and I think that's made it very strong and it means there's that constant flux between academics on the one hand, who want to theorize and problematize, and people from the community groups on the other hand, who immediately want to gather the stories and use them in community action forms. So sometimes there is a little friction, but in the end that is very healthy and it does encourage debate on both sides and encourages

ROBERT PERKS

academics to be more community-aware and community-embedded; and it encourages community activists to be more theoretical. But I think the breadth of the British oral history movement has been its strength, so my advice would be to keep your own organization very inclusive, very broad, and to pull in lots of different constituencies of people and to make it a very vibrant organization; I think that's pretty essential.

**M. V.: According to you, to what extent is it possible/recommendable to share a narrator's story, as it is discussed for example in Michael Frisch's "Shared Authority"?[84]**

R. P.: Mike Frisch's book was an important reminder that as oral historians we all work as co-creators of our historical sources and that the relationship with our interviewees is part of understanding what the interview tells us. But also that we can involve interviewees in what we do with their words. Others have written about the challenges of interpreting interview data where that analysis conflicts with the interviewee's interpretation, but at the least we now recognize the need for fully-informed consent of the whole process not just of interview but of using the material after the interview has finished. This might be a book, or an exhibition or a radio program. Where there has been discussion, it's been about how far the interviewer and the interviewee can actually collaborate equally on any given output and whether this is desirable or not. I tend to think, for example, that a radio program or a CD compilation is a creative exercise which is to a large extent a personal "artistic vision". It's tricky to involve interviewees in this directly. But vital to explain what you're doing, for whom and why, so they can listen to how you have interpreted their stories and disagree with you if they like. So it's the "how" and "degree" of shared authority that remains a challenge.

---

84) A new question for the English edition of the book. Robert Perks's answer delivered via email, October 20, 2012.

**M. V.:** How does oral history co-exist in the environment of journalists who refer to themselves as documentary-makers (if their work may be considered oral history) and the academic environment? I am asking this because some Czech so-called documentary-makers don't care much about historical accuracy or ethics towards the narrators. Has it been or is it still like this in your country?[85]

**R. P.:** Everyone is now claiming that they're doing "oral history" and often it's not something I recognize. For example is StoryCorps (and now its UK cousin, the BBC's Listening Project) "oral history"? They're "conversations" not interviews and remarkably unreflective and un-self-critical, though not without interest. But does it matter? Well, it might do when you consider how long we have been trying to establish oral history as a respectable source and methodology within the academy, where critics continue to regard oral history as subjective, loose and lacking rigor. We know that a lot of university-based oral history is none of those things but the phrase is so broad-brush that there is inevitably a lot of shallow, poor interviewing going on in the name of "oral history", which doesn't help the academic cause. It also matters because people think that oral history can be learnt in a day, when we know as practitioners that it can't, that it's infinitely complex as a source, far more so than many other historical sources. This needs to be more widely recognized generally and within academics in particular. Oral history is a set of several methodological skills: technical, interpersonal, legal and ethical, evaluative and interpretive. All need to be learned and developed with practice. And many journalists would do well to learn from oral historians.

---

85) A new question for the English edition of the book. Robert Perks's answer delivered via email, October 20, 2012.

ROBERT PERKS

## ALEXANDER VON PLATO

"Some of them have the illusion that only to archive these testimonies is a guarantee that future generations of historians will interpret these experiences in the same way we do. I think the future generations will do it for their own."

Professor von Plato is one of Germany's best-known public historians and most prolific oral historian. In 1993 he founded the Institute for History and Biography at the Fernuniversität Hagen, Germany's only oral history centre. During the 14 years he served as the institute's director, he completed 37 research projects, including two groundbreaking studies of former Nazi slave workers and of the Mauthausen concentration camp. He is also a founder and former Secretary and Vice President of the International Oral History Association. From 2006 to 2010, he served as a member of the Historical Commission of Dresden which evaluated historical documents about the bombing of Dresden in February 1945.

More recently his book, *The Unification of Germany – A World Political Power Game; Bush, Kohn, Gorbachev and the Internal Moscow Protocols*, is standard reading for journalists, educators and students. It draws on minutes from all Gorbachev talks with high-ranking politicians, and some 80 interviews of politicians such as George H. Bush, James Baker, Condoleezza Rice, and high-level staff of Margaret Thatcher and François Mitterrand among others. Similarly, his book *Hitler's Slaves* (2010) is an important study of forced labor during the Second World War.[86]

---

86) Information based on: Indiana University Bloomington. [online] [2013-01-09]. <http://www.indiana.edu/~jsp/events/1213_lecture_aVonplato.shtml>. Canada Council for the Arts. [online] [2013-01-09]. <http://www.canadacouncil.ca/prizes/john_g_diefenbaker/bm129823613775248271.htm>.

Interview with Alexander von Plato[87]

**M. V.:** I'm very glad that you have time for me to ask several questions. The first one is a very general – I would like to know if you remember the moment when you came across oral history, a method that you could use, that is important for you?

**A. P.:** I think that there are different moments. There was a moment when I met Lutz Niethammer in 1980, when I read an announcement for a project, which he organized, and then I thought it might be better to make oral history, to collect personal reports of life stories, of memories, to focus on people from below. That was one of these decisive moments, and it was at the same time when I was very unsatisfied with the history I did before. I was unsatisfied with the possibilities of a historiography which focused on political history, on economic history, on the history of governments, administrations, and elites. Though I had made a lot of historiographical attempts even about special persons coming from the resistance against National Socialism, or about refugees who left the German Democrat Republic or I have had some experiences with such people before, but I never had the view on this history as a totally different perspective, as a different dimension, which is necessary for a way to a more universal historiography, without a lack of the subjective perspective on history... You can call it "experienced history" – in German we have two words for the two meanings of experience. There is the word "Erfahrung", that doesn't mean an experience of a special event (that would be in German an "Erlebnis"), it's more a form of looking back and working through special experiences, or a special time or a life story, and then we call it "Erfahrung". I grew up on the country side after the war, full of refugees, and my family gave them accommodation, about one hundred in the first year. And about twenty years or thirty years later, some of them came back, and told us stories of their living on our farm after the war. Coming from different parts of Germany, coming even from Czechoslovakia, coming from the East, coming from different situations, separated

87) Interview with Alexander von Plato (A. P.) recorded by Miroslav Vaněk (M. V.), Lisbon, Portugal, February, 2008.

ALEXANDER VON PLATO

from their families and so on. That was so interesting, though I was – in a political sense – not always on their side, because I thought the refugees must be integrated into the western society and we shouldn't see back to the bigger Germany of 1937, and shouldn't go back to Poland. It was a political question. But the personal stories they told us, not full of revenge, not at all, it was so rich, it was a perspective which was sometimes totally different, nearly in opposition, to that what I have read about refugees before. That was the other point. And there was a third point: the development of the lefties after the student's movement 1968, some of them tried to make a different historiography, of the victims, of the suppressed, the forgotten, of those who had no chance to get in history, have no chance to be part of a historiography. Paul Thompson wrote this book *Voice of the Past*, it was an expression of that time. Give these people a voice. That was the same in Germany among the "history workshop movement".

**M. V.: I will tell Paul Thompson next week about it.**

A. P.: It was a title which was in the air. In a different sense we used it in Germany, as well. Give the people a voice in history. I think historians never like to be seen as an expression of a specific historical situation. But I know I am. I was special, but I was a part of this development. At the beginning of this movement I did not have all these ideas. But the German history and reality forced us to look at the people "below". We had a mixture of different theories, and all of them ended with the question. How could National Socialism be so successful, and what was attractive for the people? And this question was in a certain sense in contradiction to the fundaments of a history from below, because not only elites were involved in National Socialism. Oral history shows that the life even within National Socialism and under dictatorships is much more differentiated as "normal" historians think.

**M. V.: You say that they give a voice to the people, the human beings. What is the power of it? What is crucial to give the power to oral history, to open "secret" doors?**

A. P.: I think it is the subjective perspective, the power of memories, thoughts and attitudes from a former historical period to the next one, the effect of former socialization on the presence. Therefore we should make clear that oral history is not only combined with the sources of voices. In my opinion, it is a historiography of experience ("Erfahrung" in German), and therefore we must use all subjective sources like diaries, photos, photo albums, letters, and so on. All of them we have to take into consideration to get this perspective. I mean, this is a very different perspective and dimension in comparison to the "normal" historiography. And if you mean the power of this experience in history, then I would say this oral history brings us as historians to the question of the role of people within the historical process. And it's a pity that normally in the changes from contemporary to pure history, this dimension disappears. And, the power of our history is to give this dimension of subjective experience back to historiography. That's one point. The second point in the development of the history workshops and of oral history in Germany was connected with some political questions, connected first of all with the victims of and the resistance against nationalist socialism. It was connected with the demand for a democratic historiography. And we looked back to the nineteenth century to find predecessors among former historians like Lamprecht, the French "Revue" and later the "Annales", even the "historists" in Germany used this subjective source like Droysen or to Sweden for instance or to Poland, to different other countries, where inquiries of people were used to save a disappearing world, during industrialization for instance, or the early research on Indians in North America. The "traditional" historians distrusted these methods to analyze the meaning of subjectivity in history, individual or collective remembrance – even in Germany where the importance of former attitudes and the aftereffects of former political systems, just of the National Socialism or of the German Democratic Republic were and are evident; they didn't ask for any continuity in the "heads" of the subjects. These old historians who were not even positivists were in favor of a political historiography without subjects except the "big personalities" like Hitler. The critic of this historiography came up in the

1960s in Germany by historians who sympathized with the student's movement. A big part of the people who had experienced National Socialism was still alive and had to live in the new systems after 1945 in both parts of Germany. Germany is a country with I think about five different political systems in one or two generations. Lutz Niethammer said in the late 1970s, that there was until that time no research about the continuity in the consciousness of the people.[88] He initiated a project about these questions, about the influence of these former experiences on the post-war time; therefore he didn't want to make the same periodization as before. This project (called "LUSIR") dealt with the time between 1930 and 1960 and focused on these questions, how former attitudes and experiences influenced later political and personal orientations, the consciousness of generations, sexes – their differences and similarities and so on. These questions and especially the methods of oral history were not accepted in the universities even in the 1980s, not at all. Therefore a lot of people who worked outside of the universities started to work with these methods, in the trade unions for instance, one of the biggest, in a historical competition of pupils. I think oral history became a power just in the 1980s and was more and more accepted at the universities during the 1990s. I think the first colleagues doing oral history were very isolated in their country. Therefore they liked to come together at international meetings.

**M. V.: I like that too, because it is power for me.**
A. P.: Yes, but you are coming from the other side.

**M. V.: I have read your articles and heard your speeches, so I know your ideas. What would you say to Czech conservatists who only trust written documents and say that it's stupid to trust human memory since it's the worst we can use. I, of course, use all materials, and you know we are historians. I think you have experienced a similar attack by conservatists. How did you respond?**

---

88) There was one famous exception: The project "Bavaria in National Socialism", led by Martin Broszat in the middle of the 1970s.

A. P.: Yes, you are right and I wrote about it, about the question of time witnesses and historical professionals at the universities. One of the main points in the discussions about oral history is the misunderstanding that oral history is mainly a method of looking for special events, a method to reconstruct facts and figures. However, I think oral history has its main strengths in analyzing the subjective dimension, the experienced, the "digested" history by individuals, groups, generations, sexes and so on, and not the same strength to reconstruct "real" history.

**M. V.: The facts.**

A. P.: Yes, the facts and dates. But we should not exaggerate by emphasizing the contradiction between oral and written sources. To analyze the subjective dimension we need all subjective sources, not only oral ones, for instance diaries, letters, photo-albums, autobiographies and we have to confront and to compare these sources with other ones. On the other side I'm always wondering if I'm not too strict in this point. If you look at the history of historiography you see that many of very important themes and subjects were done at first by oral historians. For instance, the first research on Nazi concentration camps, of refugees in Middle and Eastern Europe, of the prisoner-of-war camps in the Soviet Union all that was based on oral sources at the beginning, then it became wider and wider, worked through by different historical approaches. Here you can see the "heuristic function" of oral history also for traditional historical approaches. Just now a project we presented here on the International Oral History conference, we can see that former forced laborers have a very good memory for details, for the factories, for the names of the masters, the colleagues, the products and so on. I was very astonished because I was skeptical asking them these concrete questions after so many years. It might be that they had to be very precise to get this compensation and prepared themselves together with others. However, I think there is more behind these good remembrances – these intensive or traumatic experiences are burnt in the memories. In addition, you cannot work only with written files because these written files are – concerning National Socialism – from the other side, from the perpetrators.

**M. V.: How do you see the future of oral history? Do you see any dangers for it?**

A. P.: I think it depends on the themes and the politics in different countries. For instance, in this case the question of recognition of the forced laborers is so different in the former Soviet Union than – let us say – in Israel, the Unites States, the Netherlands and Germany. In these countries the holocaust is burned in the history, and the forced and slave labor, the experience of concentration camps are part of the history, of the memory culture, and is part of the politics against or towards the past years. But it's very different in other countries. And therefore politics interfere in memory cultures and vice versa. And "past politics" is decisive for financing research and some regimes or governments do not have interest to allow research of their past. A second answer: We have the task as oral historians or as historians in general to save a lot of testimonies of witnesses in different forms, written or recorded on audio or video-tapes to save these testimonies of those who have the experience of the past, in Germany especially of National Socialism, of World War II, of the post war time and so on. We have just in Germany, in Israel, in the United States and in some other countries a lot of archived testimonies which can be used in future times when these witnesses are dead. In the Unites States the Visual History Archive at Yale University produced these testimonies during the last thirty years. The Spielberg Foundation filmed about 45,000–50,000 testimonies, mainly with Jews. That's different to Eastern Europe. I think some Eastern historians distrust these archives because they focused on Jews. They ask: "And what about our prisoners of war, what about our workers who were transported to Germany or what about the victims of Stalinism?" And similar questions. Today Eastern European historians ask: "What about the victims of Stalinism?" There will be a lot of themes for oral historians in all countries about any time, not only political themes. Oral history or "experienced history" will be necessary at any time to keep subjects in historiography. On the other hand, the struggles between different historical schools will continue, especially against oral history.

However, I would like to raise a fundamental problem: The next generations of historians will use our testimonies as they want to. They will present parts of the interviews and videos as they have to do it for their time, perhaps. Look at the former videos of persons in my generation, for instance leaders of the student's movement – you can't understand them sometimes, journalists have to cut the interviews and to make them understandable for later generations. In a certain sense the witnesses will be "homunculi", artificial or test-tube beings. The present time, the present generation has difficulties to understand and interpret comprehensively what generations before meant.

**M. V.: But there are differences between journalists and historians...**
A. P.: Yes, we have to show at least the context, more than most journalists do that. The next generations of historians have to contextualize all these testimonies and to comment them. As well as we have to do it today. And we have to transmit the whole life story of these time witnesses. They are not only victims, for instance, we have to show what they did before their persecution, what they did afterwards. And we have to transfer as much material as we could find. That's the task of historians. We have to be aware that we are part of this communicationalized historical process. But some of our profession has the illusion: to archive these testimonies will guarantee that future generations of historians will interpret these experiences in the same way we do or did it. I think the future generations will do it for their own.

**M. V.: I have one last question, very short. Do you have any advice for younger colleagues in the Czech Republic?**
A. P.: I think I can't give advice, because you have very different conditions than we had. Perhaps they should be more precise in methodological question than we were at the beginning, contextualize the testimonies, and put the different sources together, perhaps against each other, to see more facets of this history. If you only have the testimonies and think they should speak for themselves that would be an illusion. They have to be contextualized, they have to

ALEXANDER VON PLATO

be analyzed, and in my eyes we shouldn't publish only the testimony. There are so many different testimonies, with their own perspective that they should be set in a context by historians and of other interviews and so on. We should see the necessity of oral history as an analysis of experienced history but in the concert of other historical methods and perspectives. At the same time we have to save the testimonies of your time and to transmit them to future generations of historians.

**M. V.: I would like to ask you two additional questions. 1) In your view, to what extent is it possible/recommendable to share a narrator's story, as it is discussed for example in Michael Frisch's "Shared Authority"? 2) How does oral history co-exist in the environment of journalists who refer to themselves as documentary-makers (if their work may be considered oral history) and the academic environment? I am asking this because some Czech so-called documentary-makers don't care much about historical accuracy or ethics towards the narrators. Has it been or is it still like this in your country?[89]**
A. P.: Concerning the two additional questions: The first one I cannot answer because I do not know the concept of Michael Frisch. The second one I had implicitly answered already.

---

89) New questions for the English edition of the book. Alexander von Plato's answer delivered via email, January 9, 2013.

## ALESSANDRO PORTELLI

"A large part of the documents we find in the archives are transcriptions of things said orally and are just transcriptions over which we have no control. Or they're judicial rulings, acts of congresses, minutes of meetings – falsifications of what was said. So there's a lot to be discussed about the extent to which they are really reliable. But at least we can say they are more accurate in their data. And the point is that oral sources do different work. For this reason I'm convinced that a person doing work with oral sources must also look at the archives and printed sources."

Alessandro Portelli (Rome, 1942) has taught American Literature at the universities of Siena and Rome from 1974 to 2012. He is the Chairman and Founder of the Circolo Gianni Bosio for the critical study and promotion of people's cultures, folk music, and oral history. He has served from 2004 to 2008 as advisor to the Mayor of Rome on the city's historical memory. His works on American literature and culture in Italian include books on Woody Guthrie, Mark Twain, Washington Irving, African American literature. His books in English include *The Death of Luigi Trastulli. Form and Meaning in Oral History* (Albany, 1991), *The Text and the Voice. Speaking, Writing and Democracy in American Literature* (NY, 1994), *The Battle of Valle Giulia. Oral History and the Art of Dialogue* (Madison, Wisc., 1997), *The Order Has Been Carried Out. History, Memory and Meaning of a Nazi Massacre in Rome* (NY, 2003; winner of the Viareggio Book Prize in Italy, 1999, and of the U.S. Oral History Association Best Book Award in 2003); *They Say in Harlan County: An Oral History* (NY, 2010, winner of the Weatherford Prize of Appalachian History, 2011, and the Luigi Onofri Literary Award in Italy, 2011). He is also the author of multi-media essays (I Can Almost See the Lights of Home. A Field Work Experience in Harlan, Kentucy, with Charles Hardy, III, winner of the U.S. Oral History Association for best non-print use of oral sources, 1999) and records of field-recorded Italian folk music (most recently, La Valnerina ternana. Un'esperienza di ricerca-intervento, 2011; Mira la rondondella. Musica, storia e storie dai Castelli Romani, 2012). In November 2012 he was awarded the Luigi Tenco Award for his work in collecting, promoting, organizing and writing about folk and popular music.

### Interview with Alessandro Portelli[90]

**H. P.: First of all, thank you for giving us some of your time. My first question is when was the first time decided you to get involved with oral history, and why?**

A. P.: It was a very gradual process... Let's say that in the late 1960s, whether as a cultural passion or as, shall we say, a way of beginning some engagement in politics, I began to study the songs of working-class people, protest songs, etc. But then at the same time, in the late 1960s, 1967, 1968, one of the things a lot of young people were doing then was going into the "borghetti" in Rome. The "borghetti" were the "shanty towns" and "favelas" that were still there in Rome, the hovels. So they were going in to do social work, mostly helping children with their homework. And since I happened to be there, I started doing interviews with the people who lived there without knowing, without ever thinking about oral history or anything, just doing interviews.

Here's what gradually happened, that little by little, as I was listening to the songs, I began to realize that they almost never, especially with songs about contemporary history, about the labor movement, about the resistance – and those were the ones that interested me most – that the singers almost never sang them without telling some story. And at a certain point, since my musical education is worse than nil but since on the other hand I did have some background in literature, I began to realize that those stories were interesting. And besides that, when I realized that some of the stories contained mistakes... That's when my passion really took off: Why these mistakes? What was the meaning of these stories? We might say that in this respect things were facilitated by the fact that I am not by pro-

---

90) Interview with Alessandro Portelli (A. P.) recorded by Hana Pelikánová (H. P.), Rome, Italy, April, 2008.

fession a historian; otherwise, I might have said like so many of my colleagues that oral sources are not reliable. Instead, since I nurtured this artistic and literary passion for narrative – in literature we never throw a good story away just because it isn't true. A good story is full of meaning even if it isn't true, like a novel, right?

And so that's when I started to get enthused about this business of narrative, of historical narrative and how inside this narrative we find narrative construction, the imaginary, desires, the dream. That thing that later I learned from Luisa Passerini to call subjectivity although then I had no word for it. And so all this, I mean the work in the working-class suburbs in the late 1960s... But then my move to oral history is from the middle 1970s when I was working mostly with the labor movement, on working-class songs and politics in Terni.

**H. P.: Luigi Trastulli...**
A. P.: Yes, Luigi Trastulli. That's where it all took off; that is, when I discovered that it wasn't true that Luigi Trastulli died in 1953, and my question was: Why are these people telling that he did? Then in this sense all my work after that was just thinking... Not thinking about the interview, about oral history as a reflection of events but rather as a product of work in which memory and the imagination construct a meaning of events. Having started out from that point, it was natural then for it to happen that I wanted to do research on the history of the labor movement in Terni between 1949 and 1953. The first interview I did was with a lady who started talking to me about Garibaldi... But I wasn't even able to throw that stuff out. I mean, the whole thing suddenly fascinated me, the unpredictability of these stories, the fact that people had a lot more to tell than you could imagine being able to ask them about.

**H. P.: I am interested in knowing something more about the development of oral history in Italy in general.**
A. P.: We could say that in Italy there are two traditions. There's the tradition we could call academic although that's not really right. I mean it's not academic in the pejorative sense of the term; it is so

in the good sense of word, I mean that it is located inside public research institutions. It is personified most of all by Luisa Passerini. Luisa Passerini is the person who brought to Italy the work of Paul Thompson, the English historians, etc. There wasn't very much else in university circles in Italy. Now we have the splendid study on memories of the war, on the bombings by Gabriella Gribaudi in Naples – she's the President of the Oral History Association. And then the other camp is the one that came from militant history – beginning with Gianni Bosio. It was Gianni Bosio who went to oral sources and working-class music in the mid-1950s.

Bosio makes an important observation on the history of the non-ruling classes, the working-class world. Up until now, he says, the history of the working class has been written by thinking about the history of the controlling groups in the Communist or Socialist Parties. And he said, "Maybe we ought to go to take a look at the history of the people and also at all the other forgotten strands, at the Anarchists, at the religious Utopians, and at that segment of the working-class world that's not involved in politics, at working-class piety, at daily life. And to get to those things what is absolutely crucial is oral sources and music." And he wrote a really wonderful essay – already back then in the mid-1960s – with the title In Praise of the Tape Recorder, and there he says we have the existence of the tape recorder to thank for the fact that we can now do for the culture of the working classes – and that is mainly an oral culture – the same critical, philological work that they've been able to do on written culture. Because now we can stop discourse, re-listen, re-read, analyze. And so it was precisely Bosio who had the idea of bringing to bear on the culture of the working-class world all the philological, technical, and other competencies that had been developed for written culture. And this was one important thing.

Another starting point for reflection, for work with oral sources was Rocco Scotellaro. Rocco Scotellaro was a young poet and trade unionist from Lucania who in the mid-1970s decided to document the lives of the peasants in the South. He wrote a wonderful book on five lives of five Southern peasants. And here, we find the idea that there's no other way... I don't think that Rocco Scotellaro made recordings, no more than the other great founder in this kind of work, this militant history. I'm talking about Danilo Montaldi. Danilo Montaldi was a sociologist from Cremona. Bosio was from Mantua. Those two had no love for each other; they didn't see things the same way... And Danilo Montaldi published two very important books: *Militanti politici di base* (Grassroots Militant Politicians) in which he shows that what matters are the ordinary people inside political movements; and the other one is *Le Autobiografie della leggera* (The Autobiographies of Petty Crime). "La leggera" means antisocial petty crime, almost anarchical. This is in the early 1960s. There are all the ideas coming from critical Marxist groups like I quaderni rossi (The Red Notebooks), these being precisely the expression of the period of the 1960s, the first half of the 1960s, involving reflections on the transformations in the make-up of class, that is, what are the workers of today, what are the cities of today, thinking about the need for works of inquiry. So going out into the field, etc.

Then we can say that there is this militant strand, there's the university strand that came fifteen years, almost twenty years later. And somewhere in between these two there's the important work of local institutions, institutes for the history of the Resistance, of libraries – these being somewhere in between the militant and scholarly research strands. Well, the scholarly and theoretical contributions came in much greater volume from militant research than they did from university research. And then later from Luisa Passerini. Luisa Passerini was an isolated figure among Italian academics; she came up against great resistance from other academics. I don't know if you've interviewed her yet; you ought to. Really she was the only person doing history research in Italian universities to give a central place to oral sources. Then if we think of the other figures we have – Cesare Berman who comes from the Gianni Bosio strand and who is virtually unemployed.

**H. P.: Unemployed?**
A. P.: Yes, he doesn't have a job. And Giovanni Contini, who works for the Ministry of Cultural Heritage, that is, not at a university... I teach American literature, I am at a university, but I teach something else.

ALESSANDRO PORTELLI

Inside the universities, the teaching of the methodology and practice of oral history is practically nonexistent in Italy; I mean there's very, very little of it. I don't know if it's started up yet or if they're still discussing it – a proposal for a doctorate at Naples. I don't have any recent news about it. A research doctorate, that means something between a Master's and a PhD.

**H. P.: My next question is about your reaction to the critiques of oral history. I mean, the critics usually say that oral history is too subjective, that it can be manipulated, that it's not exact, that it can't be of the same quality as written documents...**

A. P.: The point is, if you wanted oral history to do the same things that archive documents do, then archive documents are more exact. Not always, of course, because a large part of the documents we find in the archives are transcriptions of things said orally and are just transcriptions over which we have no control. Or they're judicial rulings, acts of congresses, minutes of meetings – falsifications of what was said. So there's a lot to be discussed about the extent to which they are really reliable. But at least we can say they are more accurate in their data. And the point is that oral sources do different work. For this reason I'm convinced – but I'm not conceding – I'm convinced that a person doing work with oral sources must also look at the archives and printed sources...

**H. P.: And the ideal way of doing research is to compare everything...**

A. P.: Yes, to compare everything. But here's the point: when oral sources occupy the central position, the objective of research is not so much the minute reconstruction of events as it is in a certain sense the history of memory, the history of the construction of meaning and the history of subjectivity. Yes, it's true that they're subjective. Indeed, I would say that the kind of contribution that I've made is that of... back in those days we quoted Fidel Castro. You remember that Fidel Castro after the failure of the sugar cane harvest said that they had to turn the defeat into a victory. And that's just what I was thinking: let's transform those things that are considered shortcomings in oral sources into their strength. They're subjective. Fine. Let's work with subjectivity. Which is not the same thing as arbitrary. They are sources that have been manipulated but manipulated in the sense that just like right now, what I am saying depends on the relationship I have with you. So, fine: let's work on dialogue, on the encounter of two different subjects, O.K.? These are sources where people forget, where people are mistaken. So fine; let's work on the silences, on the things they forget, on their mistakes. And then really, after all, in my opinion, for the most part, oral sources are also accurate in their facts. Almost always. But look. The play between the various sources is just that: looking at how institutions leave records and how people leave records, at what the relationship is between these reconstructions of memory. And so to the objection that oral sources are not reliable, you can answer in first place that there are no a priori reliable sources. And in second place, that we will submit oral sources to the same verification that we require of all the other ones. O.K.? We'll crosscheck them...

And yet it's when they are not reliable that I get excited. So what is the problem? It's that to know that they are not reliable; you have to have done the work to verify the facts. That is, you have to know that Luigi Trastulli died in 1949 to be able to understand how important it is that people are saying no, he died in 1953. Because if you don't know – 1949 or 1953? – what difference does it make? Here's something I always say, a little formula I've given myself: we are doing three jobs: We're doing the normal work of a historian, i.e., trying to find out what happened. We're doing the normal work of an anthropologist, i.e., trying to find out what's in people's minds. And then we're doing the work of an oral historian, i.e., bringing those two things together. And standing in that space there. This is what I believe in. And in the sense that we don't reject the critiques but we take them as a point of departure to do a completely different kind of work.

**H. P.: What will the future of oral history be like?**
A. P.: Look, I already feel behind the times because for example I don't use video. We could talk a long time about the use of video.

ALESSANDRO PORTELLI

For example, if I were doing this interview, you would be captured; you would be in the field. Because video tends to present a dialogue as if it were a monologue. You would be in the field. There are two of us talking.

One thing today that is causing a lot of discussion by many of my colleagues is the endless possibilities opened up by digital and by information technology. Because till now, if you consider those archives [of the Circolo Gianni Bosio], one of the enormous problems of the sources was the difficulty in consulting them. All of us are building up these enormous archives. It's very difficult to consult them. Well, digitalizing them makes it possible for you to access them more quickly and in that way facilitates the idea of consulting not just the transcriptions but the original sound itself. It has become easy to reproduce the sound; it has become easy to make CDs alongside books, not instead of books: you do some things with books, and you do other things with CDs, but you put them together. For example the last edition of the book published by Fosse Adreatine comes with a CD inside it, I don't know if you've seen it. So this is something we can do. And then you can do unbelievable things. There's a program now that they showed me where you have something being filmed and a transcription of it going along together, running along in synchrony. You can do an infinite number of things.

But what we have to really guard against is letting ourselves get overwhelmed by this ideology of technology and starting to think… For example, there's one thing we don't do, at least not yet, we don't put our interviews on the Internet. We don't put the interviews on the net because it's something that can be manipulated. And then too, since an interview is a dialogue that is also pretty intimate, pretty personal, where those people are saying things but saying them to a person right in front of them, not saying them to the whole world. And so then we try to maintain a strict control over the use of these archives.

Now in the case of this interview that we're doing here, this is practically a public interview, here I'm not telling you anything personal or intimate. But in general, I mean, let's suppose, the interviews with the dissidents in Czechoslovakia, we have to pay attention to how we do them. So in this sense, this is the first reason. The second reason is the great risk that the Internet has created, and I see it in other areas to, it's laziness. That is, too lazy to work... You don't go out to do research any more, you don't go to the library and you don't go to the archives. You don't leave your own room because you've got everything on the Internet. Well, this is another risk.

But having said that, I want to add that we are working, we are trying now to construct a kind of portal for oral sources, that is, the future is there, on the technical and material level. On the level of the topics for research, it's pretty exciting because oral history – all things considered – has grown and has very strong local roots. And this in a time of globalization... Right now I'm doing research, work on a factory in Terni that is now named Thyssen-Krupp. Well, to do anything with Thyssen-Krupp in Terni now, it's fundamental to know what happened to Thyssen-Krupp in Turin. Where seven workers were burned alive. Yesterday another Thyssen-Krupp worker died in Terni. But it's also important to know that there's a Thyssen-Krupp factory in India. I've interviewed the people in India. That there's one in South Africa. Right now I'm asking friends in South Africa to interview people. Then there's one in Alabama... And we're doing a whole project in Brazil.

When I was working on the strikes in Terni between 1949 and 1953, I looked at it all through the optics of the mountain and the valley. Now you talk with those workers, and they start discussing among themselves about whether the stainless steel production in China is sufficient to cover the domestic Chinese market. The challenge of globalization is an important one, and we have followed it closely in oral history, with a lot of work on migrations. But I think one very strong topic also involves understanding that even those who haven't migrated these days still live in a global and worldwide dimension, and any research on one locality is research that involves... To do any serious research on Thyssen-Krupp, you have to have the money to go to South Africa, to go to Alabama, to India, to Germany, to France... This is the challenge of globalization.

Then too there is the fact that the forms of class conflict have changed a lot. So have our identities. And so we are, I personally am

ALESSANDRO PORTELLI

still a bit tied to the idea of social conflict that I got from my education. But it's changing from day to day. So then research should help you understand how the world is changing. But if you don't know how, if you don't have any idea about how the world is changing, you can't even formulate a hypothesis for a research project. So I think that it's a bit a question of feeling... The old projects on the identity of a neighborhood which I continue to do – yes, they're coming along nicely – but the identity of a neighborhood... We did a book on Centocelle, a neighborhood in Rome. But how can you talk about Centocelle without talking about the people who come from the Congo, from Mali, from Peru? Before it was already hard because you couldn't talk about Centocelle without talking about people who come from Le Marche, Puglia, Abruzzo. And now!? So in a word, these identities are changing. It's more complicated, but it's wonderful, lots of fun. It's a challenge...

**H. P.: What is your view on the persuasiveness of oral history? What can it provide to help us better understand the past, the present?**
A. P.: I think it can offer us so very much... Certainly the feeling of the connectedness we have with the past. Because it's clear, that is the big difference. One of the critiques of oral sources was that an archive document is contemporaneous with the facts. More or less. An interview takes place afterwards; if you interview someone in Prague about 1968, you're doing it forty years later. I think that if I want to know exactly what happened in Prague in 1968, maybe oral sources are not the first thing I go look for. But if I want to know what it means...

The interview is not a 1968 document; the interview is a 2008 document. Then what we have is a document from 2008 that is talking about 1968. So we have a document about the relationship between 2008 and 1968. So we are not thinking of memory with that somewhat positivistic and erroneous idea that memory in time only gets worse. I don't think so. Memory is not that the facts are there and we can't help forgetting them. Memory is a continuous work. The facts stay there and you keep going – more or less consciously – transforming the meaning in the course of your life, in the course of time. So what it gives us is precisely what the meaning means, what the past means in our present.

It's clear that this requires competencies in analysis and interpretation, a multiplicity of instruments. For example, Luisa Passerini has been strongly influenced by and is very well versed in psychological terminology, in psychoanalysis, etc. Others take a very strong anthropological approach. I have the tools of narration, of language: I focus my attention on the story as such rather than on the content of the story. Because back then basically at the beginning we were saying: for the sake of oral sources, we're going to interview people, we have access to their experience. But no. We have access to a story about their experience. So the fact that time comes into it, that it involves language, that it's a dialogue – all these things are elements that give a meaning to this story. And then really, it is persuasive in so far as you can prove what you're saying.

The other thing that has always excited me is that oral sources never end. In the sense that the people that you can interview about the Fosse Ardeatine mount up to three hundred, two hundred thousand in Rome. Then you can interview the same people after more time has passed. So it never ends. One of the things that oral sources do then is bring under discussion the arrogance of us who think that we are writing a definitive history, that we are consulting all possible sources. Oral sources bring everything into a dimension of tentativeness, of work in progress – which does not mean weakening it. It means transforming something stationary into something that is moving. And I think this is one of the things I find so appealing about it.

I'd like to give you an example. In the course of the last month I conducted a series of interviews in Terni, during which one of the big topics was safety in the factory. And after there were those seven deaths in Turin, almost everybody kept saying: "We here have done good work on safety. We have norms. Of course they can never be absolute, but we've done... In a word, things here are not like they were in Turin." That's what they said until yesterday. Yesterday a worker got killed there. So I'll go see them tomorrow, and what are they going to tell me? So you see what happens? Can they

ALESSANDRO PORTELLI

still say the same things about safety that they were saying a week ago?

I did interviews in 2004 but now in 2008, does what they said in 2004 still hold true? We produced a CD on the struggles in Terni in 1953, published in 2003 with the interviews done between 1979 and 1981. So we've got three different times. That is, when in 2003 we re-listened to the interviews done in 1979, 1980, 1981, we found things that we hadn't found before because in 2003, we were asking different questions of the same documents. So this stuff is always on the move. If you want to do, if you want to write a definitive book, after which no one can ever say anything more, then just forget it. I interviewed friends and family of sixty of the Fosse Ardeatine victims. There were 335 victims. I could get another ten books out of it. And in fact, there are people doing just that.

**H. P.: My last question – do you have any advice for the new Czech Oral History Association that was founded a year ago?**
A. P.: The Italian Oral History Association was founded just a year ago, too! Well, anyway, my advice is usually misguided, so... The only thing, in my opinion, is that it's important to try to keep in mind when we're doing this work that it takes a whole lot of patience. And that people often tell us things that we don't know whether they will interest us in twenty years... And that you shouldn't do this work if you don't really have a strong desire to. This is really one thing you can't do in just a scholarly or academic way. You're dealing with people. So it's like that. But I think it's you who'll be able to give us some lessons in a few years.

**M. V.: In your view, to what extent is it possible/recommendable to share a narrator's story, as it is discussed for example in Michael Frisch's "Shared Authority"?[91]**
A. P.: In the first place, these are narrators who are sharing their stories with us. On the other hand, once we are given the story, we

---

91) A new question for the English edition of the book. Alexandro Portelli's answer delivered via email to Miroslav Vaněk, November 1, 2012.

ought, when we can, to make sure that the narrators are aware of what we are doing with them. I always submit to the original narrators (when I can reach them) the ways in which I am going to quote them in my articles or publication, and accept their corrections and revisions (in some cases, when I feel that their revisions erase some of what makes the quotes interesting, I negotiate). After all, the story belongs to them!

**M. V.: How does oral history co-exist in the environment of journalists who refer to themselves as documentary-makers (if their work may be considered oral history) and the academic environment? I am asking this because some Czech so-called documentary-makers don't care much about historical accuracy or ethics towards the narrators. Has it been or is it still like this in your country?**[92]
A. P.: Basically, I think along the lines of your comment: what counts is historical accuracy and depth. Some journalists achieve it; many don't even know what it is. In the case of video, also, I think it's important for the author to take responsibility, to include making of documentary in the final version, so that viewers (or readers) will always remember that it's one person's construction and interpretation, not a slice of raw truth, as many documentaries try to appear by eliminating all traces of the interviewer.

---

92) A new question for the English edition of the book. Alexandro Portelli's answer delivered via email to Miroslav Vaněk, November 1, 2012.

ALESSANDRO PORTELLI

## DONALD A. RITCHIE

"The greatest thing about doing oral history is actually sitting down with the individual and learning about that individual, having them tell you things that they would never have told anybody else, and getting them to explain their own past and their own events. It is just a wonderful human relationship."

Donald A. Ritchie is historian of the U.S. Senate. A graduate of the City College of New York, he holds a Ph.D. from the University of Maryland. In the Senate Historical Office he has conducted oral histories, edited historical documents for publication, and provided research and reference for senators, scholars, reporters, and the general public. He has been a frequent contributor of historical commentary in the media, and has published a number of books including *Press Gallery: Congress and the Washington Correspondents* (which won the Richard Leopold Prize from the Organization of American Historians); *Reporting from Washington: The History of the Washington Press Corp; Electing FDR: The New Deal Campaign of 1932;* and *The U.S. Congress: A Very Short Introduction*. A former President of the Oral History Association and council member of the International Oral History Association, he is also the author of *Doing Oral History: A Practical Guide*, and the editor of *The Oxford Handbook of Oral History*.

### Interview with Donald A. Ritchie[93]

M. V.: I would like to say I am so pleased that you have given me your time to ask some very simple questions which could be important for our audience. As the first one, I would like to ask if you remember the first time you came across oral history, when you realized that it was so important for you.

D. R.: In my case it was very accidental. I was doing a doctoral dissertation about a man who served in the New Deal in the 1930s. I was

---

93) Interview with Donald A. Ritchie (D. R.) recorded by Miroslav Vaněk (M. V.), Oakland, USA, October, 2007.

reading through his papers, which were very traditional manuscript documents in an archive. In them, I found the last 50 pages of a 700-page oral history interview that he had done just before he died. I was astonished by it. I didn't know he had done it and I tried to find the first 650 pages. It turned out to be the last transcript that he hadn't finished correcting at the time of his death, which was the reason it was still in his papers. I finally tracked down the whole interview to Columbia University. I was in Washington DC so I took the train up to Columbia. And there were 700 pages of the man I was writing about telling me about his life in his own words. It was as if he was speaking to me. It was an epiphany. Now he didn't say everything I wanted to know. For instance, he only talked about his public life. He didn't say anything about his private life. He didn't mention his family, didn't mention any of his personal problems. At the end of his life he had gotten into trouble with his taxes and had gone to jail for not paying his taxes. These were things I really had to learn about, so I got a tape recorder and went out to interview his widow and his children and people who had known him throughout his career, including the man who prosecuted him in his tax case. All that changed the nature of what I was writing about completely. I could never have written the kind of book I did without those oral sources. Right after that, when I was applying for jobs, the U.S. Senate wanted to hire someone to do an oral history program. I had gotten that experience in graduate school. So that totally accidental experience was very beneficial in the long run. I've been doing oral history for the Senate ever since.

**M. V.: Fascinating accident. What do you think about the power of oral history? Is there something very special in this field or method?**

D. R.: Well, I usually tell people that I don't do oral history to confirm what I already knew. I do it to confound what I thought I knew. I do it to make the issue more complicated because everybody's story is a little bit more than what you would have found in any other source. By coming at it from a different perspective, they can complicate the issues. Their testimony makes it harder to write a straight narrative

DONALD A. RITCHIE

because you realize there are so many different tensions that go into any particular event and so many different perspectives on that same event. In doing my interviews, I've learned so much from those individuals. And while writing a biography, this helped me to create a three-dimensional picture of a man whom some people really liked and some hated, who was very successful in some things and a total failure in others. Oral history puts a human quality into it. At the Senate, I interview people who have worked for the institution for their whole careers. They know things that were never written down. They were in the back rooms, when the doors were closed, when the deals were struck. They were able to observe the key players, and they have very good memories of the events. They explain that what appears to be one thing can actually be something very different. In some cases it was a legislative ploy, a strategy to get something done indirectly, rather than by a direct route. So, I am constantly discovering that the story is richer than I would have been able to find otherwise. I think that's where the power comes. It's the power of the teller of the tale. The person who was there who has had direct, first-hand experience, and who has an understanding of what it meant. It may not be the right understanding. In fact, I may interview somebody who has a completely different understanding of it, but it's important to hear all those voices. A lot of those people feel that if we hadn't been doing the interviews that their voices would not be included in history, that the official voice would be listened to, but not their role in the particular event.

**M. V.: Sometimes, those who are doing oral history in the Czech Republic hear some skeptical voices about methods, especially from the conservative historians, that oral history is too subjective, that memory is selective. How would you answer these voices?**
D. R.: Those are all valid questions to rise, but my response is you have to be skeptical of every source. You need to be skeptical of written sources. A lot of memoranda in the government are written not to tell you what happened but to disguise what happened. Newspapers sometimes get stories wrong. A lot of the written sources we consult are inaccurate. Diaries are very subjective. Letters are also

subjective. So, you should be skeptical of the oral sources just the way you are of the written sources. You try to compare them against each other. When I teach, I tell students that if their written sources and your oral sources do not agree, they should not automatically believe that the written source is right. The oral source can often lead them to a better written source or can contradict what the written source said because the written source was inaccurate at the time. For instance, there are newspapers that never reported on a strike because the company that was being struck was one of their big advertisers and they didn't want to embarrass them. But if you talk to people who worked there, they can tell you that indeed there was a strike for these reasons. In the United States we have had the mainstream press but we also have had an African American press in the black community. For many years, the white press did not cover events in the black community. If you really want to know what was going on in the black community, you had to go to those black newspapers.

**M. V.: That's true. What about the future in oral history? How do you see the future for oral history, for oral historians?**
D. R.: The big change now is the technology which has changed enormously. Oral history has always been driven by technology. The availability of tape recorders after the Second World War made oral history possible as a profession. Now the availability of digital cameras and digital recorders is not only opening up the way we do the interviews but what we do with the interviews when we're finished. One of the great developments has been the use of the Internet, being able to post interviews online. For many years, I went to oral history meetings and would hear people give reports about their interviews, but I would not be able to read their interviews unless I could travel across the country to the library where those interviews were located. Now many of those interviews are being posted online where I can read and sometimes hear them. A far greater number of researchers are going to be able to use these collections. So, I see the future being much more creative in the public presentation of oral history. We'll still produce books but not just books. There will

DONALD A. RITCHIE

be more documentaries, more museum exhibits, and a lot of inter-active use of oral history. We are just at the beginning of that whole trend.

**M. V.: I have one last, almost voluntary question. Could you rec-ommend something to Czech oral historians, some advice or some message?**
D. R.: One of the things I tell students is that oral history projects have developed, over the years, standard ways of proceeding. We have ethical standards. We have technological standards. These are suggestions about how to do oral history. But the fact of the matter is that there is no one way to do it. You should try to hit the highest standards but in some cases you're going to have to be creative. You're going to have to break the rules and do whatever works in that particular circumstance because that's the only way you are going to get that interview, depending on the interviewee's decisions or whatever the other circumstances are. There are a lot of comprom-ises that go into doing oral history. My recommendation is to do what works for you. Do what has worked for you in the past, and do what works in this particular circumstance. The most important thing is to do it. Do interviews and get those people's voices recorded. There is no set formula for doing it in the long run and every rule that has been created has been broken in a creative way. Don't be afraid of it. The greatest thing about doing oral history is actually sitting down with the individual and learning about that individual, having them tell you things that they would never have told anybody else, and getting them to explain their own past and their own events. It is just a wonderful human relationship. I have met the most inter-esting people over the years. I have had wonderful opportunities to meet people. Some of them were very famous, some you have never heard of, but they had wonderful contributions to make to history. I have learned an enormous amount from them. As a historian I have gained a lot in terms of my own writing from the people that I've interviewed. I feel privileged to be able to record and preserve their interviews.

**M. V.: In your view, to what extent is it possible/recommendable to share a narrator's story, as it is discussed for example in Michael Frisch's "Shared Authority"?[94]**

D. R.: Michael Frisch makes a very important point that an interview reflects both the interviewer and the interviewee. The interviewer shapes the process by selection whom to interview and what questions to ask. Just smiling and nodding and paying careful attention during the interview encourages the interviewee to speak candidly and at length. But ultimately, it should be the interviewee's story that we are collecting, and that means listening to things we might disagree with, and questioning that information without interrupting it and arguing with it.

**M. V.: How does oral history co-exist in the environment of journalists who refer to themselves as documentary-makers (if their work may be considered oral history) and the academic environment? I am asking this because some Czech so-called documentary-makers don't care much about historical accuracy or ethics towards the narrators. Has it been or is it still like this in your country?[95]**

D. R.: Many different disciplines use interviews but not necessarily in the same ways. Oral historians usually collect life review interviews with identifiable individuals. Social scientists may use focused questionnaires to collect information anonymously. Journalists also employ interviewing in their daily work but their means of collecting and using that information sometimes clashes with oral history standards. Journalists normally seek answers to questions about a specific event or issue. Their style is sometimes adversarial. They rarely get a written agreement to publish the information. And they often do not save a record of the interview other than what gets published or broadcast. It is not that journalists cannot do good oral history; they just have to think differently about the process. Women journalists in Washington, DC, have sponsored an oral his-

---

94) A new question for the English edition of the book. Donald Ritchie's answer delivered via email, November 5, 2012.
95) A new question for the English edition of the book. Donald Ritchie's answer delivered via email, November 5, 2012.

DONALD A. RITCHIE

tory project about pioneer women reporters. At first, they debated whether to use oral historians or to conduct the interviews themselves. They reluctantly decided to hire oral historians but when one of the women reporters finished a series of interviews, which were very different from her own style of reporting, and which she found a very rewarding experience where the interviewer had helped her recall things and allowed her to speak her mind, she said, "Now I understand why we used oral historians."

## ALISTAIR THOMSON

"Oral historians are magpies, we have to grab ideas from different disciplines, different cultures, different countries to do what we do as well as we can."

 Alistair Thomson is Professor of History at Monash University in Melbourne and was previously Professor of Oral History at the University of Sussex in England. He is project leader for the ARC-funded Australian Generations Oral History Project, a national collaboration involving the National Library of Australia, ABC Radio National, the Oral History Association of Australia, and colleagues at Monash and La Trobe Universities (see http://www.arts.monash.edu.au/australian-generations/). Al's research and teaching explores the ways in which different kinds of life story evidence can illuminate the past and its meanings in the present lives of individuals and society. His books include *Anzac Memories: Living With the Legend* (1994, 2013), *The Oral History Reader* (1998, 2006, with Rob Perks), *Ten Pound Poms: Australia's Invisible Migrants* (2005, with Jim Hammerton), *Moving Stories: An Intimate History of Four Women across Two Countries* (2011) and *Oral History and Photography* (2011, with Alexander Freund). Website: http://profiles.arts.monash.edu.au/alistair-thomson/.

# Interview with Alistair Thomson[96]

**M. V.:** I am glad we are meeting today. The first question I would like to ask is when was the moment you encountered oral history? Do you remember when you felt this would be your way?

**A. T.:** I do. I have a very vivid memory of that. I was an undergraduate historian at Melbourne University and we were doing a course about Australia between the two world wars and I discovered that the year 1919 after the First World War was the most violent year in white Australian history, when the soldiers came home, back from Europe. An extraordinarily contested year. And I became interested in what happened when the soldiers came home (we knew a lot about the Australian soldiers during the war). So I thought why don't I go and ask old ex-servicemen, First World War veterans, not about their war experience, but about their coming home experience. And so, for an undergraduate project I went to the Returned Services League, which is an ex-services organization, in a working class suburb near where I lived in Melbourne and said, "Can I interview some of your members about their experiences coming back to Australia after the war?" They gave me some names and I rang up these people and wrote to them. The first one was a man who lived by himself named James McNair. I turned up to interview James McNair, I knocked on the door and he opened it, and he was there, he was resplendent in a silk dressing gown and he led me directly to the whiskey cabinet where he had a bottle of whiskey and he poured a drink and he poured me one, which I didn't drink, but I put there. And then, for the next several hours, he was just astounding because his memory was really sharp and he was a wonderful singer and he sang songs from the war and he talked about coming home and how difficult it was and what the challenges were. I went home just buzzing with adrenaline. It was so exciting. Every time I've interviewed ever since it's that same excitement.

My most recent interview, because I haven't done that many as I've been teaching oral history, my most recent interview I did a

---

96) Interview with Alistair Thomson (A. T.) recorded by Miroslav Vaněk (M. V.), Guadalajara, Mexico, September, 2008.

ALISTAIR THOMSON

couple weeks ago. We've got a new project that we are piloting in Australia about everyday life in Australia in the 20th century. I did this interview with a man, again in the inner suburbs of Melbourne, and it's the first interview I've done since I came back to Australia. And it was just wonderful, I just loved it because it was a five, six hour life history interview and there was time to relax and get this man's story and relate it to the themes of the project but also to find out all the complicated ways that lots of factors in people's lives shape their life story and their trajectory. Education, family, class, gender, and how you can get a rich sense of that through the interviews, but also how important it is to listen to the really idiosyncratic and personal and intimate details because it illuminates the bigger picture. James McNair was my first interview and this man, we haven't got permission yet so I can't tell you his name, this man who I interviewed a couple of weeks ago is my most recent interview. And it was the same just really rich pleasure of having this man unfold his life story before me, but being an active part of that and actually helping him to develop and tell his story and asking questions about things he hadn't thought about and then he would think, "Oh yeah, that's interesting, yea maybe," and being part of that, being part of enabling someone to tell his story, being part of the process, like Václav Havel in your video when he says, "The story you get from me when you interview me will be better than the one if I write it down because of the dialogue." Being a part of that dialogue is very exciting.

And then I think all of the histories I've ever done have been micro-histories which start with individual stories but works out to how we understand bigger stories, as history starts with individual stories. There are all sorts of issues with that. How do you generalize from one or a number of stories? And how do we do that analytically and all sorts of issues? But actually I do it because I think it's intellectually significant and provides important things to historical understanding. But if I'm really honest I do it because I enjoy listening to people tell their stories. And I could go back, I mean it's probably about my family background and being partly brought up by a grandmother who'd had an extraordinary life and enjoying listening to that, and so I think I like listening.

**M. V.: My second question is about the power of oral history. What is so important about it?**

A. T.: What is so important? I think there are several reasons. I think that the starting point for oral history when it took off again in the 1960s and 1970s was about, well, whose stories are not recorded in the archive. We've moved a long way from that and we do it for a lot of other reasons, but I think that is still a fundamental motivation. It's thinking about which stories, not just whose stories, but what stories, what aspects of historical experience are less likely to be on the record and therefore we can create a record because otherwise there will be important missing chapters in the history. So I think even though we've moved on a long way to all sorts of other things, I think that's still of continuing significance.

I think it was Michael Frisch who made the argument that we've moved to a point that memory is not just the source of history but the subject of history. And I think probably the second reason why oral history is so valuable is not just that it's research about the past, it's research about the past in the present. In individual lives, but also in the way individual life stories respond to, and draw upon, and react against public narratives, and to changes in their lives. So whenever we are conducting an interview, it might be about James McNair in 1919, but really it's also about James McNair in 1983, when I did the interview, and it's about all the things that have happened ever since. So really what I'm doing, which came up in the last session of this conference, I'm exploring his memory biography, which is a phrase I used when I wrote Anzac Memories. What is the way that his memory and his articulating his life story has developed and changed over time up to now? And what can we learn about 1983, and how Australian society made sense of this First World War experience, and how somebody like James McNair made sense of it in terms of his changing life experience, and how his ongoing and contested and negotiated relationship with the public narratives? So that's the second reason.

So one, it's about unrecorded stories, two it's about memory as a subject as well as a source, and three? Three and four connect, but three is about empowerment and four is about advocacy and I

ALISTAIR THOMSON

think they're connected. Three, it was my colleague Joanna Bornat in England who put this pretty well, she said that there was a moment in her oral history career when somebody turned around and said after the interview, "Thank you for interviewing me." And Joanna realized that actually the people we interview get enormous value out of this process, the fact that someone is interested in their story and that their story is of historical significance can be tremendously affirming. Particularly if you've been silenced in one way or another, and a feeling that you are getting your story on the record, so I think that on a very personal level the third value of what we are doing is that it makes anybody feel like their story is significant. Both for themselves, and wider.

And that connects to what I believe is the fourth value of oral history, which is that just in the same way as it can be empowering for an individual, it can be an empowering thing collectively. Because if there's a group of people's stories, for example people with disabilities, and I'm thinking of doing a project with colleagues in Australia looking at an audiovisual history of the deaf community in Australia, a community who have been silenced in a whole range of ways. And for each of those individuals telling their stories through Australian sign language is empowering, but collectively as a group recognizing that they've a collective story and then making that public to other people, making their story public impacts on the public narrative, on the public histories of our society. And then there is that important effect that when you put a silenced voice into the public narrative in the way that women's history has done or disability history more recently, then suddenly all the individuals who felt their story was not significant begin to think it is. The best example I had was when I first started doing oral history in England in the mid-1980s working in a community history group, and turned up at a working class house to do an interview with members of the family. And the women, we were actually doing a project on working class women, and the women would say, "Talk to my husband Joe, he knows about history." There was a sense that a working class woman's life story was not of historical significance. That's not true anymore. Because there has been so much oral history work done just in Brighton, in

England where I lived, that working class women know that their stories are history. And so they won't say go interview Joe, they will say "Yes I've got a story which is important," and they've been affirmed, and it's one of the great successes of oral history that there are lots of groups of people now who see themselves as historical subjects. In television, in exhibitions, on radio, and feel like their stories matter. So there are probably other reasons, but those are four really important ones.

**M. V.: I would like to know if you have a problem with our conservative colleagues, mostly historians, these critics who speak about subjectivity and bad memory. What would you say about that?**
A. T.: Well you sigh and your shoulders sag because you've been arguing this stuff for 25 years. The first thing I say is, "OK, you are a medieval historian and you don't trust, you think my oral history is unreliable. What would happen if you could go back in a time machine and bring a medieval person to 2008 and interview them, would you say no? Of course you wouldn't say no because it's a wonderful opportunity." That would be my first response. My second response would be the one that oral historians used right from the start. That every source that we use is problematic in different ways and a large proportion of sources that historians use are story sources of one form. They are people giving evidence in court, they are people writing letters, writing diaries... all of those accounts are shaped by the subjectivity of their narrator. They are shaped by the time of the telling, to use Portelli's phrase, and the languages and meanings available at that time. They are shaped by the genre of storytelling, the police/court context, how do you write a letter, all those things. And actually, they are also shaped by retrospectivity, because many of them are not writing about the moment in which they are writing it. They are writing in a police court reflecting about something that happened a year ago, as evidence, so retrospectivity has already happened. And I suppose one of my responses is: The time of the telling of any account is significant because of a) the subjectivity of the narrator in relation to the story they are telling and b) the public narratives which remain in relation to that story. It

ALISTAIR THOMSON

is always shaped by those two things. And whether it's shaped fifty years later – and yes you've got more changing in both subjectivity and public narrative over time – but even the letter that's written at the end of the week talking about a week ago is shaped by the retrospective position of it. So what I would say now, and I feel much stronger to say this now than I ever have, that actually oral historians can teach other historians to look more critically at their sources because we've been subject to criticism so long, we've become, with people like Portelli and others, so acutely sensitive to the issues about our source and have developed methodologies and ways of understanding and working with it that I think that we can actually go back to the other historians and say, "Learn from us about your sources." So that would be my other response, but my first response is to say, "You know you have a chance to interview a Roman gladiator, would you say no? Of course you wouldn't."

**M. V.: I remember well the situation in Sydney about the discussion of the future of oral history, about globalization, Internet, modern technology... what do you think about the future of oral history?**
A. T.: It depends where you go on that one. I mean do you want to talk about internationalism or digitalization?

**M. V.: Digitalization, probably.**
A. T.: I'm probably not the best person to ask. Because I'm not very technically adept. My family laugh when I say I've got a new recorder because I can't work the video machine at home. One thing that struck me is that the digital age in one sense is a sort of apotheosis, a sort of victory in that anyone, anywhere can now record their story, in digital storytelling online, and so on. In one sense that's wonderful. In one sense, through blogging and through the Internet, that lots of people now have a sense that their story has value, that they can put it down, record it and send it out to anyone anywhere. And in one sense that's a great victory for oral history because we are a part of that autobiographical age which has encouraged people to realize that individual stories are important. On the other hand you could say it's problematic because oral history becomes redundant. Who

needs oral historians when everyone can tell their story now. I'm doing a funding bid at the moment where we have to respond to that criticism because I know people will say, "Why do we need to give you a million dollars to do this oral history project when we can just scan the web and collect the stories through that." And one of my responses is that there's a great difference between the multitude of stories on the web and what we do in oral history. Because when we do an oral history project we support and structure the storytelling and give it some sort of focus and theme. It becomes a dialogue where we interrogate, in the best possible way, people's memories and push it forward. And then importantly we archive it and we make it available under clear conditions with consent so that other people can use it. It's like a structured storytelling. It's a dialogic and structured storytelling that is thematic and therefore is more readily useful by researchers and historians and others. So I think that's a value and therefore I think there will be a continuing value to have someone on this side of the microphone, where you are, interviewing me. I don't think if I were sitting there talking to myself into my webcam, I don't think I'd have the same conversation. The dialogue is very important and the fact that you've got six questions and the fact that you've done the same six questions to a whole lot of different people and then we can look comparatively across them.

Your first question was about the importance of oral history. Another importance of oral history is that it is multimedia by definition, and it enables us to make engaging oral histories in a whole range of media. And if you look at oral history, you know, television history, radio exhibitions, dance, all those things, it just enables a way of working with the past and present through different media. That is tremendously exciting and whether you are doing audio interviews or video interviews, each of them enables you to create wonderful products that people will engage with, and perhaps the digital native population that grew up with digital stuff and are more comfortable with digital technologies than old-fashioned books, this will be the way they want to do their history. Which actually means that in oral history we've got a head start.

**M. V.: Do you feel oral history is a method, or more like a field?**

A. T.: I don't know. I think that oral history is a field, an approach. I think it's a movement actually, that would be more appropriate. In one sense it's a methodology, or a set of methodologies. I don't think it's a discipline, I don't like the notion of calling it an academic discipline because I think disciplinary boundaries are problematic. They set boundaries...

**M. V.: It is said that there are two branches: academic, and voluntary or educative, but not from the academic sphere.**

A. T.: Most of the work I've done in the last 25 years has been to try to break that down. Another great thing about oral history is that it happens in the academy, but actually, certainly in Australia and Britain, most oral history happens outside the universities. It happens in community based projects, reminiscence work, theater projects, radio projects, museums and so on, and the academic stuff is fairly marginal. One of our great challenges is how do you bring those two together. So all the wonderful thinking about theory and method in oral history which often happens in the academy connects to all the wonderful projects and engaging approaches that are happening outside the academy. I'm trying to bring those two together. An important thing about oral history is that it does enable that kind of connection. Paul Thompson, in The Voice of the Past, made that argument: It helps us bring together the academy and those outside, as makers as well as users of history.

**M. V.: The last question. Do you have any recommendations for Czech oral historians? We are still at the beginning of this movement...**

A. T.: That's a good question. You are running the conference in Prague and the reason lots of us will come to Prague is to learn from your experience and learn about doing oral history in post-communist Eastern Bloc countries and what have been the challenges and opportunities and innovative things that you do. One of the reasons the international movement of oral history is so exciting is because you learn from difference and different parts of the world.

We also appreciate similarities and the two things together are very exciting. In terms of lessons, I think that lesson about making sure, working out how to combine the academic and outside the academic world would be a very important lesson. And as part of that, that real challenge of combining thoughtful theoretical ideas about memory, about interview relationships, about technologies, all that sort of thing, combining that... The reason it's so important, the academy needs to learn from what is happening outside the academy, but also the academy needs to learn from the wonderful thinking and ideas that happens within. That would be one. The other lesson is to listen and hear beyond your own national context, or your own regional context and think about what can we learn from somewhere else. The worst mistake in oral history was when we had cassette recorders and you would do one side of the recording and then you would turn the tape over, and then you would turn it over again and wipe out the first side. So if you want a lesson, we've all done that at some point. Another thing: training. There is a terrible thing that happens in most history departments that they say if Joe wants to go out and do interviews, he can just go out and do interviews. And I say that that is appalling, because actually you can teach for a whole semester a course on doing interviews and at the end of it the students realize they have learned a lot, they realize how complex it is and how many skills and approaches they can learn. So having good training, at whatever level, is really important, I think.

**M. V.: You have been involved in the International Oral History Organization now for a good number of years. For the last two years you served as President. How do you see the way the institutionalized movement of oral history has developed over times, and where do you see it is going?**
A. T.: I think it is really important thing because this is a movement, as an institution, or pre-institution, which developed in the 1970s with a group of colleagues in North America and Europe who came together in Europe in the 1970s and continued to meet as a group of colleagues. And that was tremendously important. I went to the conferences in Oxford and Essen and Italy and so on through

ALISTAIR THOMSON

the 1980s and into the early 1990s, but it was a group of friends who were getting older, a generation that was getting older and to their credit they realized that they needed to institutionalize this so that it will have continuity and that it will be democratic. The founding of the International Oral History Organization in 1996 was a really important part of that process, and due credit to the founders, the pioneers, who didn't keep it to themselves, they created this association. Ron Grele did the constitution and they created a democratic organization, and I think they made some very important decisions. One of which was that the conference every two years would move around the world because previously they had all been in Europe. That was very important because it has exposed European and North American oral historians to work around the world, but it has also done the reverse, it has exposed different parts of the world to Europe and North America. So I think it has truly become in the last decade a much more international movement through that which is very valuable. The main aim is to keep having this meeting. Another thing is the real challenge that there are really wonderful, important literatures about oral history from different countries and different languages exposing the different methodologies and politics in the various places, and unless you speak those languages, unless pieces are occasionally translated, you really don't learn from them. I really don't know – I've got a sense of what has been significant in Latin American oral history, which has been, like Eastern Europe, over the last 20 years, a very important site for new thinking, new politics and approaches. Because I don't speak Spanish or Portuguese, I don't really have a sense of that. I think working out a way as a movement that we can ensure that some of the most important thinking, the most novel approaches that happen in different parts of the world come through, get translated into English and Spanish, maybe through Words and Silences so that we can share those literatures and really learn, not just from being at this conference but also through reading online. And also to disseminate them beyond the association to others, to our colleagues who are skeptical about oral history, to see that there is this rich interdisciplinary and international and multilingual literature about this field of work. That's another thing that is exciting about oral history, it is interdisciplinary; it's not just historians, it's anthropologists, people working in museums, people in social psychology, linguistics. At this conference there is a whole range of people, and that's another really exciting thing. It forces you outside your narrow boxes as an historian, exposes you to literatures and approaches from a whole range of different disciplines and makes you an intellectual magpie. You have to grab ideas like a magpie, the bird which steals objects and brings them together in its nest. Oral historians are magpies, we have to grab ideas from different disciplines, different cultures, different countries to do what we do as well as we can.

**M. V.: In your view, to what extent is it possible/recommendable to share a narrator's story, as it is discussed for example in Michael Frisch's "Shared Authority"?**[97]

A. T.: Concerning this question I will refer to my previous article concerning this topic Moving Stories, Women's Lives: Sharing Authority in Oral History.[98] Here I only mention my basic findings concerning "shared authority" as experienced during my oral history research with four women on the main topic "moving" – their stories about moving (emigration after the 2nd World War) from Great Britain to Australia. As oral historians, we offer people not only a chance to tell their life stories; we also offer them an opportunity to become a part of history – in a form of texts or books we produce as final research outputs. And our narrators are conscious of it. Because of this, shared authority between interviewer and interviewee should make an indispensable part of the research – that was my point of view in the mentioned project with women. I tried not only listen to but also understand women's interpretations. I proposed my version of their lives and asked them to comment (or correct) these outputs. In this form of work, a historian is confronted with discrepancy between his responsibility towards history on one side and towards

---

97) A new question for the English edition of the book. Alistair Thomson's answer delivered via email, October 25, 2012.

98) Moving Stories, Women's Lives: Sharing Authority in Oral History. Oral History 39 (2), 2011, pp. 73–82.

ALISTAIR THOMSON

narrators on the other. Compromises here are inevitable. Finding a "right" balance in this process of "shared authority" usually helps us to know more from "our" narrators.

**M. V.:** How does oral history co-exist in the environment of journalists who refer to themselves as documentary-makers (if their work may be considered oral history) and the academic environment? I am asking this because some Czech so-called documentary-makers don't care much about historical accuracy or ethics towards the narrators. Has it been or is it still like this in your country?[99]
A. T.: Good question. I think journalist interviewers operate with different aims and different ethics – there has been some recent writing on this, in I think the US Oral History review.

## PAUL THOMPSON

"If you have the chance of interviewing someone who has quite a bit to say, don't just stick to your agenda. Of course, ask the questions you want to know, but also be willing to divert onto other things."

 Paul Thompson is Professor Emeritus in Sociology at the University of Essex and a Research Fellow at the Young Foundation. He is Founder-Editor of Oral History and Founder of the National Life Story Collection at the British Library. He is a pioneer of oral history in Europe and author of the international classic *The Voice of the Past*. His other books include *The Edwardians* and *Living the Fishing*. He is co-author of *Pathways to Social Class* and *Growing Up in Stepfamilies*, and most recently, *Jamaican Hands across the Atlantic*.

---

99) A new question for the English edition of the book. Alistair Thomson's answer delivered via email, October 25, 2012.

## Interview with Paul Thompson[100]

**M. V.:** Thank you again for your kindness in meeting and for inviting me to your house. It's a great day for me because I have read a lot of your works, and you are like some god for me. I didn't know anything about oral history and the first book we got in our oral history centre in 1995 was the second edition of The Voice of the Past, I think. I would like to ask you two questions: The first one is a little bit difficult; if you are the father of oral history I don't know how I can ask when and where you came upon oral history. Do you remember the moment when you first used oral history?

**P. T.:** I sometimes think about what were the very first influences that led me towards oral history. Strangely enough I think that one of them might have been that my grandfather had his own Pentecostal church. One of the ideas of Pentecostalism is to let people speak and give testimony to their faith, and in church you have to listen to everybody, however strange they may seem to be, as when they are "speaking with tongues". There is just a possibility that that idea was there in the background.

More certainly, I came to oral history for two reasons. One was becoming a socialist and feeling that the experiences of ordinary people and what they thought was important. The other was more specifically that when I went to Essex University I went to the Sociology Department because the History Department didn't exist yet. The founder of that was Peter Townsend, a great sociologist and champion for the poor and the old in this country. He had just finished a notable book on The Family Life of Old People in East London – as it happens in the same part of London as we are in now. He carried out many in depth interviews for that book and he was very struck by how old people had vivid and interesting things to say about their former years. I was already a social historian and he kept showing me this material and said that I should think of using it or collecting it. So he put the seed in my mind.

100) Interview with Paul Thompson (P. T.) recorded by Miroslav Vaněk (M. V.), London, Great Britain, March, 2008.

PAUL THOMPSON

Then in around 1966, I was commissioned by Eric Hobsbawm to write the volume for 1900–18 in a series of social history of Britain of which he was acting as the overall editor. So Peter and my other colleagues said, "Well there are a lot of people still around from the early 20th century, there are all these people who remember that time, you should go to interview them." I wanted to follow the same kinds of themes as sociologists were investigating about contemporary British society in general, looking at the experience of working class families, at work and at leisure, and personal relationships, in terms of age and gender: issues that were not part of the political record but dealing with day to day life. I was very lucky in that, it was at that time extraordinarily easy to get research money for innovative work, and we were generously backed first by Nuffield College, Oxford, and then by the newly-established Social Science Research Council. We were given funding to record 600 people right across Britain, but in the end I cut it down to 450 and I never actually used 450 for my own writing. When I wrote *The Edwardians* the book was based only on 100 interviews. But that was the start.

When we started, we saw our method as using interviews for social history and we had not heard the phrase "oral history", but then very quickly within a matter of months we had made contact with oral historians in the United States. Although that name stuck, the name "oral history", we did not then gain a lot methodologically from this first contact. American oral historians were then primarily archivists and much more interested in great men than ordinary people's lives, although this has greatly changed since then. So we didn't get much from their practice and it was really from sociology and anthropology and other social historians that we worked out how to do oral history.

The other thing I discovered particularly after I had been asked by Keith Thomas, a great social historian himself of course, to write *The Voice of the Past*. I wanted to find out what was the history of oral history and I discovered of course that it went right back to the Greeks and that in Britain it went back to the dark ages and the monastic historian Bede. So there was a very lively tradition running for over a thousand years, and with our own innovations we were re-discovering practices which had been there before.

**M. V.: *The Voice of the Past* was first published in 1978. Was it something that you felt you had to tell to listeners, or was there someone asking for the book?**
P. T.: I was asked to write it by Keith Thomas. He was a very creative social historian himself and saw that oral history was important. But interestingly, he wanted me to write an entirely philosophical book, not one which had anything practical in it. And I insisted that the book included the practical chapters, and I think that's been a major reason for its success. It combines the two, thinking about oral history and also how to do it.

On that point, it is interesting that in a similar way, with *The Edwardians* I found myself at odds with Eric Hobsbawm. He didn't like my use of oral history at all and he asked me to cut out most of it, in particular the section with series of portraits of families illustrating the social layers of British society. He didn't like that at all. And later he went around making speeches against oral history. That was strange and disappointing because when I was writing my thesis about the Labor movement in London I felt a great admiration for his work. He seemed to be by far the most insightful labor historian and I could not understand why it that he couldn't make the leap to supporting oral history was. But he didn't.

**M. V.: It's my other question: we had a lot of problems in our own beginning with oral history. Under communism, you couldn't use it because you were under the control of the communist regime. I thought that after 1989 there would be a bigger movement in the oral history, that we would use it much more. I think it's maybe an inheritance of the Hapsburg monarchy culture that there are a lot of positivistic conservative historians who mainly refuse oral history, stressing problems with memory and other issues. They prefer written documents because they thought that they held the real truth – maybe you know these debates. I would like to ask you what your answer is to the voices which are too skeptical of oral history.**

PAUL THOMPSON

P. T.: I think at the beginning it was particularly necessary to argue that retrospectively memory has got a value. That was partly because of my being in social science, where researchers rely to a huge extent on interviews; but they think that retrospective interviews are particularly unreliable. In fact, when you start looking at the processes of memory you realize that the kind of self-censoring and forgetting and inventing and so on affects the immediate memory as much as long-term memory. When you think about social mobility for instance, when people are asked about their sequence of work, their jobs through their lifetimes, this is retrospective evidence, but strangely researchers of social mobility don't seem to be aware of general debates about the nature of memory.

As soon as something is labeled retrospective memory, social researchers thought, "Oh well we can't believe that." So we had to show the memory process and how a lot of memory was reliable in a factual sense. Then there was a second stage, which really came around the late 1970s, when people like Louisa Passerini and Alessandro Portelli started to argue that there was a double strength in oral history, that the distortions which occur in memory are actually the evidence of changing consciousness and are valuable in themselves. That is the opinion which I hold myself. Actually, the second edition of *The Voice of the Past* had a whole new chapter on "Memory and the Self" and it was in response to that. Does that answer your question?

**M. V.: Yes.**

P. T.: In terms of what people think now, I would say that in this country that oral history is accepted by most history departments as having validity and the position I always argue for – that oral evidence should be evidence evaluated just like other evidence – I think that would be the position of the majority of historians now. I'm not saying all. And it is also very interesting how in both anthropology and sociology you get a lot of use of the oral history approach, although quite often under the title of life stories. I think the shift to interest in questions like identity has meant that the life story or oral history approach becomes central to the issues that are being researched. It has been a big transformation since the time when I started out.

**M. V.: Thank you. I have a very general question. Where do you see the power of oral history? What is the story, what do you think is the power of oral history?**
P. T.: Well, I think it has different kinds of power. There is an intellectual power, in that you can show what happened, in some instances in ways which are very significant. For instance, the use of oral testimony to document the holocaust or to document the oppression by the Soviet regimes. In many cases there simply weren't written documents which show that kind of thing, and those are histories which have enormous significance even now; and that is an example of the intellectual power of oral history.

Then there is an individual power of giving self-confidence and a sense of self-worth to people. And that's being used quite widely with old people, for example those who are in physical or mental difficulties or depressed, to give them confidence and courage.

Then also, something in between those; you get the power of oral history in communities. I don't know how far this is true in other countries but we have a very interesting situation here in that history is enormously popular, it is one of the most popular social activities. It's not only local history because great numbers of people go to cathedral and country houses and so on. But local history has tremendous appeal and in most communities you find people, often not particularly educated, who are historical experts on something. For instance, in the village in Essex where I partly live there are people who know all about every boat that was launched in the river, they can tell you when it was built and where it sailed to and who it was owned by, all these things, extraordinary remembered knowledge. It is learnt partly orally, partly from documents, but the extent of their knowledge is formidable and can make me feel very inadequate as a social historian.

There are also collectors of photography who know exactly what particular photos show or the people in it and they can date it and so on. Collectors of postcards. So you have these experts, you have them in the community. I also think there's a wider sense that the community's history is part of its pride. You get terrific support for local projects and there is a whole scheme supported by the government for community oral history projects from the Heritage Lottery Fund.

I've been involved in a number of these. And when we held meetings for showing photos and extracts for our interviews there was a tremendous turnout of older people and great excitement in the interval, the talk, the positive talk was absolutely tremendous. Now I know that there has been cases in communities which were under threat, for instance for road buildings or something like that, where getting an oral history project going and publishing the book, has galvanized people towards successful resistance. So it really does have power at a community level. Our project book has sold over a thousand copies in a population under 10,000, in a local shop. I think it's really quite remarkable.

**M.V.: I don't know. I still cannot answer it based on my own experiences. What do you think about the future of oral history? How do you see future steps or the development of it? What it would be?**
P. T.: Well, I mean it's always difficult to imagine that things will be quite different from what they are now but almost certainly they will be. I hope it will continue as a form of academic research and also community work. I think the most interesting challenge in many ways is how oral historians are able to relate to the new technology. I guess that in the long run, the idea of separating the audio and the visual is becoming less and less credible, so that's part of the change to come. But, on the other hand there is also going to be more and more pressure to use the Internet. We've put our project, I mean the book was one form of publication but we also had about three times as much material edited and placed on the Internet. I don't know how much is used but it is being used. We'll see, I am slightly skeptical if these kinds of archives are really used. And then there is also the work by people like Karen Worcman in Brazil. She and colleagues in the U.S. probably have been trying to develop Internet life stories where you have sites where people put their life stories on. And again, I think that this is an interesting experiment but we

have yet to see what comes of it and how much is used. But I'm sure that in some form or other those new technologies will be an important part of the future.

**M. V.: I think there are a lot of advantages; but there are some things I am quite afraid of. If you remember the process between the interviewer and the interviewee, the narrator, with a camera you can do an interview with another person across the ocean. Is it still oral history without human contact, without the aesthetic face to face, like we are doing, if you only see through the camera, which is directed at some angle to your face?**
P. T.: The situation where the interviewee can see the interviewer or not? Can the interviewee see the interviewer?

**M. V.: Yeah.**
P. T.: Well, as long as someone can see you.

**M. V.: I will be in Prague and someone will be in Sydney.**
P. T.: I think that it's an interview, but it's not going to have the same potential closeness and feeling, is it? I know that from radio interviews when you're in a different place.

**M. V.: I prefer to have the human touch and human contact. It's much better for progress in the interview. So, I am afraid of this, if the human action could be replaced by some modern technology. If it happens, I will be a little bit sad about it.**
P. T.: I think that at a certain point the technology transformation may be able to provide a cheap and easy way of simultaneous translation of interviews. If that did happen, this would be an enormous breakthrough and would enable us to create international comparisons and connections in a way that we've never been able to.

**M. V.: As a recommended and very famous author and father of oral history could you give some advice to the young Czech Oral History Association, to Czech students who are taking classes of oral history?**

P. T.: Well I think that it's very difficult without knowing what has already been done in the Czech Republic.

**M. V.: I know, but generally, if you see some mistakes which you did or the Oral History Association did.**

P. T.: Well, one mistake I did make when I started was to be a little bit too narrow in what I was trying to do in an interview. With *The Edwardians*, with that big survey of interviews for instance, we only asked people about their lives up to 1918. We were recording these interviews in the early 1970s and we never asked about what happened in the intervening 50 years. Now, failing to do that was a very serious mistake because it meant that there were all sorts of things that we could have asked of those people that we failed to ask. Just to give you an example, I later became interested in people who grew up in stepfamilies. We had quite a few in that Edwardian set but we didn't know what had happened to them afterwards and in order to make it interesting and valuable we needed to have that information. So I think that it's always good, if you have the chance of interviewing someone who has quite a bit to say, firstly, don't just stick to your agenda. Of course, ask the questions you want to know, but also be willing to divert onto other things. Secondly, I think it's much better to have a life story interview rather than one which just focused on a particular period of somebody's life.

**M. V.: Thank you. And maybe the last question, it is the last question. Can you say what oral history brought to you personally, how it influenced your life?**

P. T.: Well, it has brought me an incredible rich professional life in which I have got to know people of a great variety, in a way that I wouldn't have possibly if I had stayed as a conventional historian or become a statistical sociologist. I have met very different people through each of my projects and a few have become long-term friends. For instance through research *Living the Fishing* in the 1970s I met a working fisherman who became an intellectual colleague in the shaping of the book and who remains a close friend I see regularly. Similarly, through recording elite interviews with pioneer researchers I have encountered personally people with challengingly creative minds; through researching *City Lives* I have got behind the facades of the financial world, finding empathy again in those sorts of interview, and again, I think that's a real privilege. I feel as a whole I've just been so lucky that I've spent a lot of my research time listening to people rather than sitting in a dusty old archive which is the way I started.

But I think it's more than that because it alters your relationship with other people in the world in general, because you have developed the skill of getting people to talk. And, I mean, although I'm a relatively shy person, I'm not so shy as I used to be and I am able to get into conversation, sometimes with rather powerful effect. For instance, Elaine Bauer, with whom I wrote one of my last books, *Jamaican Hands Across the Atlantic*, she's Jamaican-Canadian. But I met her on a Eurostar train from London to Paris. We started talking and it was like a kind of oral history experience and we have had a very very close relationship ever since then. That was the sort of thing that wasn't possible for me before. I feel very lucky in the number of friends and the variety of friends and I think that's been brought to me in a large measure through oral history.

**M. V.: In your view, to what extent is it possible/recommendable to share a narrator's story, as it is discussed for example in Michael Frisch's "Shared Authority"?[101]**

P. T.: I think we have a basic responsibility with all those we record to follow oral history ethical rules. With a minority of interviewees who are interested we can discuss with them the development of the interpretation of their own interview and the project more generally. With elite interviews with pioneer academics this is an expectation on the interviewee's part. However, I don't think most people would want such sharing imposed on them; it's generous of them to agree to be interviewed and we shouldn't try to push them into being quasi-academics. Also I think when it comes to it, in deciding the

---

101) A new question for the English edition of the book. Paul Thompson's answer delivered via email, October 19, 2012.

shape of a book or program or what is to be quoted from an interview, the initiative has to remain with the intellectual initiator of the project and to pretend otherwise is self-deception.

**M.V.: How does oral history co-exist in the environment of journalists who refer to themselves as documentary-makers (if their work may be considered oral history) and the academic environment? I am asking this because some Czech so-called documentary-makers don't care much about historical accuracy or ethics towards the narrators. Has it been or is it still like this in your country?[102]**

P.T.: As to journalists, of all types, they are not bound by ethical rules, nor can they even be trusted to keep within the limits of the law, as the phone hacking scandal in this country has vividly revealed.

---

102) A new question for the English edition of the book. Paul Thompson's answer delivered via email, October 19, 2012.

# 4/ Rules and ethics of oral historical research must be respected

These then were my interviews with prominent figures of oral history. Nearly five years have passed since September 2008 when I recorded the last of my series of interviews in Guadalajara, Mexico. Much has happened in that time and, as indicated by the additional questions to my narrators, the themes and problems of oral history that we are speaking of, that interest us and that we need to resolve continue to change. One of the relatively "new" themes is the increasingly greater degree of oral history's use in former Eastern Bloc countries and the related problems that are typical for this region.

An increased interest in oral history in our country and in all of former Central and Eastern Europe is certainly generating a sense of satisfaction and gratification to all who had, over the years, pushed for its practical application and broader use. This certainly does not mean that, having argued our position (successfully, in my opinion) in discussions with the more conservative parts of the community of historians, we should "rest on our laurels" and not see the new problems related, above all, to the very concept and use of oral history or to identifying with its principles. I consider these to be both ethical and methodical principles, meaning that a mastering of methodical skills and knowledge of the context are both a necessary prerequisite for high quality historical interpretation.

Like the South African historian Sean Field, I ask myself whether the recent boom in the use of oral history is an exclusively positive trend.[103] Is everything passed off today as oral history really oral history? I am in agreement with Alex Lichtblau and Mario Böhm[104] in

---

103) Field, Sean: *From Stepchild to Elder: Has Oral History Become "Respectable"?* February 15, 2009. http://www.iohanet.org/debate/index.php.
104) Böhm, Mario: *Oral History Revisited – Mündlich erfragte Geschichte im Journalismus.*

that I presently see a problem and threat in some of the simplifying journalist-documentarian approaches of self-styled oral historians as well as various memory institutions that are (as in most Eastern European countries) frequently ideologically motivated.[105] We should now pose the question of whether in many cases these are still initiatives (organizations) merely collecting, recording or organizing the individual memory, or if these are initiatives formulating the individual and collective memory in the spirit of the currently prevailing neo-liberal concept. Unfortunately, some of these newly created memory institutions interpret the recent past tendentiously (just like prior to 1989, except now its in the other direction) and in disregarding the narrators' rights with a blatant sensationalist angle.[106]

Given this, it is somewhat difficult for me to identify with the view of several oral historians who view it in a positive light that the spectrum of the historiography community includes, in addition to experts, academics and lay historians, also journalists.[107] This kind of

---

Diplomarbeit, Universität Wien. Fakultät für Sozialwissenschaften Betreuer 2009. http://othes.univie.ac.at/6465/.

105) Many self-styled documentarians had understood that oral history is a fashionable term these days and partially opens doors to various grant possibilities, i.e. funding. They therefore largely take advantage of it. Unfortunately, their approach is a far cry from the work of oral historians – with regards to both professional preparation and, above all, questions of ethics.

106) The latest example from a number of very problematic approaches (which unfortunately sometimes call themselves oral history) can be seen in the documentary film *Killer by Profession* (Vrahem z povolání – about a Czech military prosecutor taking part in the political trials of the 1950s), which, according to the filmmaker, was created using recordings of the narrator's life story. The interviews were allegedly authorized, although authorization in this regard is a moot point. I'm convinced that the narrator was not at all aware of the reason he was being recorded. I also do not know whether he would have been willing to give his life story if he knew that the film's title would be a judgment of his life. Unfortunately, "data gathering" scenarios like this are not a rare occurrence in the Czech milieu. Such documentary exploits clearly violated ethics. In some cases the narrators try to discontinue the collaboration, in some cases they sue, but they usually don't have the energy required for these activities given their advanced age. The Czech Oral History Association, in accordance with its goals, which includes cultivating the method and ensuring that the methodological, methodical and ethical standards are adhered to, devotes itself to such cases and tries to help narrators defend themselves.

107) Archive of the Oral History Center of the Institute of Contemporary History. Interviews collection. Interview with Robert Perks recorded by Miroslav Vaněk, Oakland, USA, October 2007.

declared "democratic trait" causes and will continue to cause significant problems. This appealing democratic nature is more like to be perceived positively by the younger generations of British and American historians than those in the Czech milieu, where only in the last twenty years has the difference between "equality" and "egalitarianism" been clarified. The journalist (or radio or television reporter) might come up with an extremely valuable story on a certain person, group of people or profession, but that doesn't mean that what he or she is doing is oral history. Even if the investigative journalist gathers information using his or her own erudition, approaches and methods, these are not the approaches and methods that we would currently (we don't dare anticipate the future in this area) mistake for oral history (or place such methods higher or lower than oral history in categorizing various professions). They are just different. They have different goals, different objects and readers, listeners or viewers than those that the results of the work of researchers in oral history or of oral historians themselves are designated for.

All the collected interviews with leading experts in the field of oral history show that, in basic theoretical and practical questions (regarding the future as well), we concur with the international trend in the field. Although Czech oral history agrees in the basic questions with the rest of the world (the meaning and value of the results, the accepted views), on closer inspection we see a few nuances in which Czech oral history differs. Some of these concern methodology and it is probably only a matter of time before our approach harmonizes with the methods known in countries with historical continuity, meaning those countries that did not experience major social upheavals or reversal (this concerns, for instance, the conducting of "confrontation interviews").[108]

However, in the Czech milieu, as in other former Eastern Bloc countries, the fact that the terms *movement, revolutionary character*

---

108) Plato, Alexander von: Zeitzeugen und historische Zunft. Erinnerung, kommunikative Tradierung und kollektives Gedächtnis in der qualitativen Geschichtswissenschaft - ein Problemaufriss. *BIOS* 13, 2000, p. 22. Cf. Vaněk, Miroslav: Those Who Prevailed and Those Who Were Replaced. In: Ritchie, Donald (ed.): *The Oxford Handbook to Oral History*. New York – London, Oxford University Press 2008, pp. 37–50.

and *oral history* are mentioned can pose a problem. The history of the connection of these words stems from the history of oral history itself, meaning from the way history was written and from the change of perspective on the "nameless" masses, whose influence began to be gradually taken into consideration – on both a "collective" (e.g. of nations, classes and professions) and individual level. Oral history went through a similar development in America and Great Britain (as well as in Italy and partially in France). From the very beginning there was obvious greater interest here in the "working classes" and social history. This was related to, among other things, the considerable influence of Marxist thinking among the intellectuals there (often even members of communist, proletariat or socialist parties) as well as to the rich tradition of labour history.[109] Even the OHA conference in Oakland in October 2007 bore in its title the adjective revolutionary: The Revolutionary Ideal: Transforming Community through Oral History.

The term *movement*, also linked to the expression *revolutionary character*, clearly takes on a political meaning in the Czech milieu and does not express a professionally determining attribute. Even our own contemporary history has shown us that a *movement* generally does not have only cognitive goals, but also social and political ones, as well as those implicitly of power, that not only is it generally geared toward achieving its goal, but is, in its integrality, directed against its opponents. It is therefore clear that this *revolutionary character* will always only be perceived in the Czech milieu within a context of the field itself in that we consider the research approach (all participants have the same chance to express themselves) and unbiased judgments that avoid a black-and-white vision of events to be *revolutionary*.

If I am (after all my experiences with the former regime), on the one hand, against political activism in research, I more than welcome intellectual activism and active means in seeking new themes and original interpretations. I have in mind here the shift in our

---

109) Vaněk, Miroslav - Mücke, Pavel: *Třetí strana trojúhelníku* (The Triangle's Third Side) ... c.d., pp. 30–74.

attention to social groups that were (and once again are) overlooked (and not only in Czech historiography) – e.g. to the aforementioned "common people". I feel that, if these groups are not re-integrated into history, the interpretation of our recent past, focusing mainly on victories and, to some degree, on defeats, will continue to be incomplete, black-and-white and, essentially, inaccurate. They say the most spine-chilling aspect of being a historian is to see that some processes repeat. It does not matter now whether this concerns the advocacy of a single proper vision of the world or the means by which this goal is achieved. What is problematic, however, is that it seems as though nobody sees (or wants to see) how such movements are, from both a historical and everyday perspective, counter-productive, short-winded and disastrous.

It seems to me that, within the context of these questions and outlined problems, Czech (and not only Czech) oral history faces an arduous task – to resist ideologizing views and perhaps even attempts at an interpretation of history that is often remote from reality. This does not only apply to oral history, but to contemporary history as a whole. I hope that all my fellow historians and social scientists enjoy the best possible condition for truly unbiased and free research, void of the infringement of any ideologies – the very thing we so vocally called for in the "year of miracles", 1989. I would very much like to see this unbiased research be assisted by published interviews with people who stood at the beginning of oral history or who are advancing our field around the world.

# Bibliography

Allen, Barbara: *Re-creating the Past: The Narrator's Perspective in Oral History.* The Oral History Review (OHR), Vol. 12 (1984), pp. 1–12.

Benmayor, Rina: *Latina Feminist Group, Telling to Live.* Latina Feminist Testimonios, Durham: Duke University Press, 2001.

Benmayor, Rina – Skotnes, Andor (eds.): *Migration and Identity.* Somerset, N.J: Transaction Pub., 2005.

Böhm, Mario: *Oral History Revisited – Mündlich erfragte Geschichte im Journalismus.* Sien: Diplomarbeit, 2009.

Dunaway, David – Baum, Willa (eds.): *Oral History: An Interdisciplinary Anthology.* Walnut Creek (California): Alta Mira Press, 1996.

Ecker, Maria – Ellmauer, Daniela – Lichtblau, Albert (eds.): *Renée Wiener. Von Anfang an Rebellin.* Wien: Die Geschichte einer jüdischen Widerstandskämpferin, 2012.

Ferreira de Moraees, Marrista: *IOHA's Tenth Anniversary. Institutionalization and Expansit of Oral History: 10 years of IOHA.* Words and Silences, Vol. 4, No. 1/2 (Nov. 2007–2008), pp. 5–21.

Freund, Alexander: Oral History in Canada: A Paradox. In: Klaus-Dieter Ertler – Hartmut Lutz (eds.), *Canada in Grainau. A Multidisciplinary Survey of Canadian Studies after 30 Years.* Frankfurt am Main: Peter Lang, 2009, pp. 305–335.

Frisch, Michael: *A Shared Authority Essays on the Draft and Meaning of Oral and Public History.* State University of New York Press, 1990.

Colman, Gould P.: *Oral History – An Appeal for More Systematic Procedures.* American Archivist, Vol. 28 (1965), pp. 79–83.

Grele, Ronald: *From the Intimate Circle to Globalized History.* Words and Silences, Vol. 4, No. 1/2 (Nov. 2007–2008), pp. 28–31.

Grele, Ronald: *Envelopes of Sound: Six Practitioners Discuss the Method, Theory and Practice of Oral History Testimony.* Chicago: Precedent Publishing, 1975.

Gubrium, Jaber F. – Holstein, James A.: *Handbook of Interview Research: Context and Method.* Thousand Oaks: Sage, 2002.

Hall, Jacqueline D.: *You Must Remember This: Autobiography as Social Critique.* The Journal of American History, Vol. 85 (Sept. 1998), pp. 439–465.

Hamilton, Paula – Shopes, Linda: Introduction: Building Partnerships between Oral History and Memory Studies. In: Paula Hamilton – Linda Shopes (eds.), *Oral History and Public Memories.* Philadelphia: Temple UP, 2008, pp. 7–27.

Koleva, Daniela (ed.): *Negotiating Normality.* Everyday Lives in Socialist Institutions. Transaction Pub., 2012.

Kvale, Steinar: *InterViews: An Introduction to Qualitative Research Interviewing.* Thousand Oaks – London – New Delhi: Sage Publications, 1996.

Lichtblau, Albert: *Ursprung und Transformation.* Leben und Werk der Malerin Charlotte Lichtblau / Origin & Transformation. Life and Art of the Painter Charlotte Lichtblau. Graz, 2005.

Lichtblau, Albert – Kirchmayer, Birgit (eds.): *Marko M. Feingold. Wer einmal gestorben ist, dem tut nichts mehr weh.* Eine Überlebensgeschichte. Zentrum für Juedische Kulturgeschichte, 2012.

Lummis, Trevor: *Structure and Validity in Oral Evidence.* International Journal of Oral History, Vol. 2, No. 2 (1983), pp. 109–120.

Mosnier, Joseph – Milwood, Beth (eds.): *Interviews from Community Voices Oral History Project: 1998–2001.* Greensboro, N.C.: Greensboro Public Library, 2010.

Morrisey, Charles T.: *Beyond Oral Evidence: Speaking (Con)structively about Oral History.* Archival Issues, Vol. 17, No. 2 (November 1992), pp. 89–94.

Morrisey, Charles T.: *Riding a Mule Through "The Terminological Jungle": Oral History and Problems of Nomenclature.* OHR, Vol. 12 (1984), pp. 13–28.

Morrisey, Charles T.: *Why Call It "Oral History"? Searching for Early Usage of Generic Term.* OHR, Vol. 8 (1980), pp. 20–48.

Moss, William W.: *Oral History Program Mannual.* New York: Praeger Publishers, 1974.

Moss, William W.: *The Future of Oral History.* OHR, Vol. 3 (1975), pp. 59–67.

Nevins, Allan: *The Gateway to History.* Boston: D. Appleton – Century, 1938.

Niethammer, Lutz – Plato, Alexander von (eds.): *Wir Krigen jetzt andere Zeiten: Auf der Suche nach der Erfahrung des Volkem in nachfaschistischen Ländern.* Bonn, 1985.

Niethammer, Lutz (ed.): *Lebenserfahrung und kollektives Gedächtnis. Die Praxis der "Oral History".* Frankfurt am Main: Suhrkamp, 1985.

Niethammer, Lutz: *Wozu taugt Oral History?* In: Prokla – Zeitschrift für politische.

Passerini, Luisa: *Work, Ideology and Consensus under Italian Fascism*. History Workshop Journal, Vol. 8 (1979), pp. 82–108.

Perks, Robert – Thomson, Alistair (eds.): *The Oral History Reader*. First Edition. New York: Routledge, 1998.

Plato, Alexander von: *International Oral History on the Move*. Words and Silences, Vol. 4, No. 1/2 (Nov. 2007–2008), pp. 21–24.

Plato, Alexander von: *Zeitzeugen und historische Zunft. Erinnerung, kommunikative Tradierung und kollektives Gedächtnis in der qualitativen Geschichtswissenschaft – ein Problemaufriss*. BIOS, Vol. 13 (2000), pp. 5–46.

Plato, Alexander von – Leh Almut: *Ein unglaublicher Frühling. Erfahrene Geschichte im Nachkriegsdeutschland 1945–1948*. Bonn: Bundeszentrale für politische Bildung, 1997.

Plato, Alexander von (ed.): *Studien und Berichte, Band 1 der Reihe "Sowjetische Speziallager in Deutschland 1945 bis 1950"*. Reihe hg. von S. Mironenko, L. Niethammer, A. v. Plato (Koordination). Berlin: Verbindung mit V. Knigge und G. Morsch, 1998.

Plato, Alexander von (ed.): *Die DDR in der Erinnerung, Studienbrief der Fernuniversität*. Hagen: Hagen, 1999.

Portelli, Alessandro: *Going against the Grain*. Words and Silences, Vol. 4, No. 1/2 (Nov. 2007–2008), pp. 25–27.

Portelli, Alessandro: *The Death of Luigi Trastulli and Other Stories: Form and Meaning in Oral History*. State University of New York Press, 1991.

Portelli, Alessandro: *The Battle of Valle Giulia: Oral History and the Art of Dialogue*. University of Wisconsin Press, 1997.

Portelli, Alessandro: *The Order Has Been Carried Out: History, Memory and Meaning of a Nazi Massacre in Rome*. Palgrave Macmillan, 2004.

Portelli, Alessandro: *They Say in Harlan County: An Oral History*. Oxford University Press, 2010.

Ritchie, Donald A. (ed.): *The Oxford Handbook of Oral History*. Oxford UP, 2011.

Ritchie, Donald A.: *Doing Oral History*. New York: Twayne Publishers, 1995.

Robertson, Beth M.: *Oral History Guide*. Umlet: AOHA, 2006.

Vorländer, Herward (ed.): *Oral History: Mündlich erfragte Geschichte*. Göttingen: Vandenhoeck u. Ruprecht, 1990.

Stone, Elizabeth: *Black Sheep and Kissing Cousins: How Our Family Stories Shape Us*. New Brunswick: Transaction Publisher, 2008.

Thomson, Alistair: *Four Paradigm Transformations in Oral History*. Oral History Review (USA), Vol. 34, No. 1 (2007), pp. 49–70.

Thomson, Alistair: *Anzac Memories. Putting Popular Memory Theory into Practice in Australia.* Oral History, Vol. 18, No. 1 (Spring, 1990), pp. 25–31.

Tompson, Paul: *The Voice of the Past: Oral History.* New York: Oxford University Press, 1978.

Vaněk, Miroslav (ed.): *Obyčejní lidé..?! Pohled do života tzv. mlčící většiny. Životopisná vyprávění příslušníků dělnických profesí a inteligence.* [Normal People...?! A View of the Life of the So-called Silent Majority. Biographical Narrative of Workers and the Intelligentsia.] 3 vol. Praha: Academia, 2009.

Vaněk, Miroslav (ed.): *Mocní? A bezmocní? Politické elity a disent v období tzv. normalizace. Interpretační studie.* [Winners? Losers? The political Elite and Dissent during Normalization. A Biographical Interview.] Praha: Prostor, 2006.

Vaněk, Miroslav: *Those Who Prevailed and Those Who Were Replaced: Interviewing on Both Sides of a Conflict.* In: Donald A. Ritchie (ed.), *The Oxford Handbook of Oral History.* Oxford UP, 2011, pp. 37–50.

Vaněk, Miroslav – Mücke, Pavel: *Třetí strana trojúhelníku. Teorie a praxe orální historie.* [The Triangle's Third Side. Theory and Practice in Oral History.] Praha: Fakulta humanitních studií UK, Ústav pro soudobé dějiny AV ČR, 2011.

Vansina, Jan: *Oral Tradition as History.* University of Wisconsin Press, 1985.

Yow, Valeria: *Recording Oral History.* Thousand Oaks: Sage, 1994.

# Miroslav Vaněk
# Around the Globe
## Rethinking
## Oral History
## with Its
## Protagonists

Published by Charles University in Prague
Karolinum Press
Ovocný trh 3–5, 116 36 Prague 1
Czech Republic
http://cupress.cuni.cz
Prague 2013

Editor Vice-rector Prof. PhDr. Ivan Jakubec, CSc.
Edited by Petra Bílková and Martina Pranić
Layout by Zdeněk Ziegler
Typeset by DTP Karolinum
Printed by Karolinum Press
First edition in English

ISBN 978-80-246-2226-2